MW00680884

Music Worth Talking About

• • • • • • • • • • • • • • • • •

Music

WORTH TALKING ABOUT

A Guide for Youth Leaders

Tim and Patty Atkins

Baker Books
A Division of Baker Book House Co
Grand Rapids, Michigan 49516

© 1995 by Tim and Patty Atkins

Published by Baker Books
a division of Baker Book House Company
P.O. Box 6287, Grand Rapids, MI 49516-6287

Printed in the United States of America

All rights reserved. No part of this publication may be reproduced, stored in a
retrieval system, or transmitted in any form or by any means—for example,
electronic, photocopy, recording—without the prior written permission of the
publisher. The only exception is brief quotations in printed reviews.

Produced for Baker Book House with the assistance of The Livingstone Corporation.
David R. Veerman, James C. Galvin, Linda Chaffee Taylor, project staff.

Library of Congress Cataloging-in-Publication Data

Atkins, Tim.
    Music worth talking about : a guide for youth leaders / Tim and Patty
Atkins.
        p.   cm.
    Includes index.
    ISBN 0-8010-0240-0 (pbk)
    1. Music in Christian education. 2. Discussion in Christian education. 3.
Music and youth—United States. 4. Popular music—United States. I. Atkins,
Patty. II. Title.
    ML3920.A87   1995
    261.5′7—dc20   95-107836

Photo Credits:
    Susan Ashton *photo courtesy of The Sparrow Corporation, Brentwood, TN, and Atkins-
        Muise and Associates, Nashville, TN.*
    Ray Boltz *photo courtesy of Paul Scribner and Ray Boltz Ministries, Muncie, IN.*
    Steven Curtis Chapman *photo courtesy of The Sparrow Corporation, Brentwood, TN,
        and Creative Trust, Nashville, TN.*
    Mark Lowry *photo courtesy of the Ward Group, Nashville, TN.*
    Rich Mullins *photo courtesy of Reunion Records, Nashville, TN.*
    Petra *photo courtesy of Atkins-Muise and Associates, Nashville, TN.*
    Michael W. Smith *photo courtesy of Reunion Records, Nashville, TN.*
    Wayne Watson *photo courtesy of Atkins-Muise and Associates, Nashville, TN.*

Acknowledgments

• • • • • • • • • • • • • • • • • •

We have always been impressed with musicians and curious about how that moment of magic comes about when a song is born. Initially, it appears the music and words write themselves, merely using the artist as a channel; however, this happens only to geniuses every fifth generation. Here's to the guys who wrestle over every note and nuance. Your efforts are duly noted.

Thanks to Eric Cherry, Ed Kilbourne, Joe Ricke, Kevin Mac-Dowell, Ken Castor, Doug Beutler, and Tim Tedder for showing up and playing live. You guys give us an up-close, live-and-in-concert angle.

Thanks to Bob Dylan, Cat Stevens, James Taylor, Harry Chapin, Bruce Hornsby, Dan Fogelberg, and Jim Croce for the first act.

Thanks to Larry Norman, Randy Stonehill, Margaret Becker, Charlie Peacock, Kim Hill, Susan Ashton, Michael W. Smith, Amy Grant, and Steve Camp for giving us the songs that inspire us with the presence of Jesus.

Thanks to Theard, Federspiel, Owens, Sell, Fast, Ester, and Niccum for Fridays at 6:45 and being the first to love the change that music can bring.

Thanks to T. C. B. Y. G. for letting us turn the sound up and the lights off.

Thanks to "Going Public" for lending an ear.

Thanks to Phil and Jean O'Shaughnessy for the love of reading and learning.

Thanks to God who gave the music and put it in the soul of everyone.

Introduction

• • • • • • • • • • • •

Music pervades our culture. We hear it in our cars, in stores, in the dentist's chair, and even on the phone. We find ourselves singing snatches of songs over and over. We have been soothed by music. We have been inspired by music. We have even been incited by music.

Like any popular medium, modern music is not without controversy. Debates have raged for centuries regarding what music is "good" and what music is "bad." Most recently, music's ability to influence our actions has been debated in our courts and legislatures. The argument has even reached Christian circles as we fight over "Christian" music and "secular" music.

Regardless of the outcome of these debates, we cannot turn off the steady stream of music; millions of people tune in to various styles of music every day. The question is, are they listening to what they are hearing?

This book is designed for use with youth groups, Bible studies, Sunday school classes, and similar groups; it is intended to help you and your group practice the art of listening. It encourages an examination of the lyrics to determine the artist's intent. It will allow your group to view the message of a song from a biblical perspective. Finally, it will help your group distinguish truth from falsehood in music and apply the truth to their daily lives.

Above all, we hope this book will get you listening—really listening—to the music that you hear every day. That music influences the way people around us think and act. Unless we know what it is saying, we cannot counteract its negative messages and emphasize its positive ones.

Song Selection

The songs selected for this book were written and/or recorded by a variety of artists. Some appeared on Christian music labels; others come from mainstream rock charts. We do not presume to label any of the songs Christian or non-Christian, good or bad—that is up to you and your group to decide. The songs were selected for a variety of reasons; some were chosen for their positive messages, others for the myths they perpetuate, still others are included simply to stimulate thought and discussion. As you choose songs to use, keep these reasons in mind.

Obtaining the Music

The names of the artist (or group) and songwriter, the album title, label, and year of release are included with the song titles. Many of the songs reached the high charts at one time or another and can still be obtained at music stores. If you don't have the song yourself, ask your family and friends to check among their old albums. You can also check out your local library; many have extensive music collections. Finally, don't overlook secondhand shops. Most larger cities have shops that deal in new and old records and CDs.

Playing the Music

Listen to the music before presenting it to a group. Having the words written out and in front of you will help you discern what the artist is saying. You may want to give the words to the group so that they can follow along as they listen. The "Crank It Up" sections give some background information about the song as well as the suggested themes for discussion.

Give careful thought to when you play the music. Some songs work best as starters to get the group thinking; others are more appropriate for the end of a meeting. You may even choose to play songs at different points in a meeting.

The Discussion

Discussion questions are included in the "Talk It Up" sections to get your group talking about the song. They also lead into the

Bible study portion, which we call the "Look It Up" section. There are no right and wrong answers to any of the questions. Discussion may take your group off in an entirely new direction. Different people interpret the same song in different ways. Respect those differences and don't be afraid to follow the direction of the conversation if it seems likely to be interesting *and* helpful.

Wrapping the Meeting Up

The "Wrap It Up" sections are simply our ideas for applying the messages of the songs. As we said above, you may view the song differently. Use the insight your group has gained from the discussion as a basis to wrap your meeting up.

Related Songs

A "Follow It Up" section concludes the treatment of each song, listing additional music that could reinforce the message of the preceding section. These can be used at any point in the meeting, or as music during refreshments, for example. They may also be excluded entirely from the meeting or simply mentioned to the group for those who wish to explore the topic further. Follow-up songs that are listed separately in this book have a star next to them.

We hope you enjoy using this book as much as we have enjoyed researching and writing it. The process of reviewing and selecting songs evoked a lot of memories for us—from the first single we bought ("Jeremiah Was a Bullfrog," by Three Dog Night) to our first Christian album (the self-titled *Love Song*). Music has been an important part of our lives, even though neither of us can play or sing a note! So whether it's Dylan or Grant, Foreigner or Petra, we have simply learned to appreciate God's gift of music. We don't want anyone to miss it.

All by Myself

Eric Carmen (Carmen)
Eric Carmen
Rhino Records
1975—*Reached number 2*

Crank It Up

When we are young, we think of ourselves as invincible and independent. We don't need anyone for anything. We think this ability to exist untouched will continue throughout our lives. But there comes a day when we realize our need for others. This Eric Carmen classic is about that specific moment. We hear his wisdom as he thinks back and sings, "Those days are gone."

Talk It Up

- Who were some of your friends during grade school?
- What things did you once think were important that are not important to you now?
- What makes people change the way they view themselves?
- Do you dislike being alone? Why or why not?
- Is your family important to you? Why or why not?
- When was the moment you felt you had grown up? Did your parents relate to you in a different way?

Look It Up

1 Corinthians 12. Why is it important for us to stay involved with other people? What happens to the body when one part quits functioning?
Matthew 18:20. What does this verse teach about Christians getting together?
James 5:19–20. How can we benefit from others?
Psalm 37:23–29. What does God promise to those who follow his ways?

Wrap It Up

"I can do it myself!" When a child utters those words, it is a sign that he or she is growing up. The ultimate goal of learning is to be able to know or do things by ourselves, to gain independence and self-reliance. Our society places a high premium on independence, so we encourage children of the earliest ages, "Go ahead, try it by yourself."

Along with this message, however, we also subtly communicate the impression that seeking someone's help is a weakness. So we tend to go through life telling ourselves that we don't need anyone. This just isn't true. As far back as creation, human beings have demonstrated the need for companionship and support. God created Adam and put him in the middle of the garden. But in spite of the splendor of Eden, God saw it was not good for Adam to be alone (see Gen. 2), so God created Eve.

The need for others does not stop as we leave childhood behind. But determination to retain one's independence prevents people from accepting help from others. Some people view religion as a crutch for the weak. How ironic that by being independent they prevent themselves from being whole. They deny themselves the most basic element of survival—the love of God.

As Christians, we need to portray ourselves as strong, independent people who still need to lean on God's love. When we demonstrate our need, others will feel free to share their needs with us. "All by Myself" are words of independence. They are also words of loneliness.

Follow It Up

"Big Man's Hat," Charlie Peacock
"I Will Be Here," Steven Curtis Chapman
"Hymn," Noel Paul Stookey

All That You Have Is Your Soul

Tracy Chapman (Chapman)
Crossroads
Elektra Entertainment
1989

Crank It Up

This is a story of a young girl who fell in love with a man who put her to work in his home, having babies and keeping house. Looking back on her experience, she counsels us to never "give or sell your soul away, because all that you have is your soul."

Talk It Up

- What's the value of all the stuff you own?
- What kinds of things have been either stolen from you or taken and not returned? How did it feel to know you would never get them back?
- What does the woman in the song mean by "giving your soul away"? Did she give her soul away? How?
- Are there any activities or relationships that are tempting you to compromise your values or standards?
- What does the songwriter mean by saying, "Don't be tempted by the shiny apple, don't you eat of the bitter fruit"?
- Do you think you can keep from making the same mistakes Tracy sings about? How?

Look It Up

1 Peter 2:11. Peter says that sinful desires war against the soul; what do you think he means?

Mark 8:36–37. How does this passage apply to Tracy Chapman's song? Does it add any insight? How do we maintain our soul?

Wrap It Up

In today's world, much emphasis is placed on discovering one's true self, one's soul. Men and women seem increasingly intent on finding ultimate truth within their own souls, believing that only then can they escape pain and experience their full potential. Many rely on crystals, meditation, and spirit guides to possess their souls. Unfortunately, the whole movement misses the boat. We don't own our souls. God, the Creator of souls, is the owner. Power is not in our souls but in the Creator who fills them. Our task is to connect with the Creator to protect us from giving in to the pull of outside forces.

Follow It Up

"Material Girl," Madonna
"Life's Been Good to Me," Joe Walsh

# Angry Young Men

Randy Stonehill (Stonehill)
Love Beyond Reason
Myrrh Records
1985

Crank It Up

We have been given an inaccurate depiction of how a Christian should act from the media. A quiet, controlled man in a collar with a soft voice talks calmly about the death of a close friend. He barely changes his expression and tone of voice as the conversation switches to controversial world issues that would bring rage in a normal person. This professional Christian seems to be lacking any common range of emotion. A more accurate depiction of how Christians should act is given in this song. How should we respond to the ugliness of our world: racism, physical abuse, divorce, violence, drug trafficking? With fire in our eyes and our jaw set firmly against evil. Jesus charges us to not turn our heads but to face the issues straight on with anger that motivates us to change wrong to right.

Talk It Up

- What's the maddest you've ever been?
- What do you think Randy means when he sings about "fire in their eyes"?
- What things make you angry? How do you show your anger?
- Is it wrong to be angry? Why or why not?
- What are some things you think Christians should be angry about? How should we show our anger?

Look It Up

Ephesians 4:26. How can we be angry and not sin? Why should we settle things "before the sun sets"?

Matthew 21:12–13. Was Jesus' anger acceptable? Why or why not? Do you think he would react in a similar way to some things today? If so, what?

Matthew 23:1–33. Jesus pronounces seven "woes" on the Pharisees in this passage, calling them snakes, vipers, and hypocrites. Do you think Jesus was angry when he spoke these words? Why or why not? If he were to speak seven woes today, what do you think he would say?

Wrap It Up

Anger can be a destructive emotion. It sparks actions and reactions that are often violent and deadly. Yet of all the emotions, anger is the one that propels us into action. One of the most commonly heard phrases following a burst of anger is "that makes me so angry, I ought to . . ."

Christians ought to experience peace and contentment, but that doesn't mean they should be apathetic and lazy. It is far too easy to move within our Christian circles, filling our spiritual bellies and twiddling our spiritual thumbs. But such behavior is contrary to the example Jesus set. The three years of his ministry were ones of constant motion. He did not turn a blind eye or deaf ear to any issue of the day. And he did not simply speak out on the issues, he acted on them. He healed the sick. He cast out demons. He drove the money changers from the temple. He was passionate about God's Word.

When Randy Stonehill speaks about "fire in their eyes," he brings to mind a man with great passion, poised for action. When was the last time you felt that way about anything? When was the last time you were driven to action? Is God inspiring you to anger—and action?

Follow It Up

"The Dark Horse," John Fischer
"Signs," Five Man Electrical Band*

At Seventeen

Janis Ian (Ian)
Between the Lines
Columbia Records
1975—Reached number 3

Crank It Up

This song was very popular because everyone knows what it feels like to want to be someone else. Throughout high school our insecure feelings control us so that we begin to "invent lovers on the phone" and "cheat ourselves at solitaire." This feeling is intensified even more if we can't keep up with our peers physically, socially, and mentally. "At Seventeen" covers the gamut of pain we feel at that awkward stage.

Talk It Up

- What age do you wish you could skip? Why?
- What's your most painful memory of being left out?
- What feeling does this song give you about high school?
- What does Janis mean when she talks about "inventing lovers on the phone"?
- Have you ever pretended to be someone you're not?
- What other pain does Janis sing about? When have you felt like that?
- Why should we worry so much about what others think of us?

Look It Up

Romans 12:2. Does this verse offer any solutions to the problems raised in the song? If so, what?
Romans 15:7. What does this verse say we can do to help build each other up?

Psalm 147:3; Matthew 11:28–30. What promises does God give us? What promises can we give God?

Wrap It Up

Peer pressure is not only someone jeering at you to do something wrong. It is also evident in how we tie our shoes, what style of clothes we wear, how we talk, and even what we do for fun. True, there is freedom of choice, but the range of choices is narrowed by the standards of our peers. All is well and good when our natural selves coincide with the "pressured" choices. But often our natural selves conflict with the choices the group wants us to make.

The truth Janis Ian learned at seventeen was that it is impossible to take our natural selves and change them to fit unrealistic standards. Her words ring with depression and pain. It is too bad that Janis did not discover that God created our natural selves for a purpose. The only standard he sets is that we love him back. How could we have taken something so simple and made it so complicated and difficult?

Only with God's love can we learn to love ourselves as we are. Only when we accept ourselves will we stop putting the pressure on others to conform to an unrealistic standard. Jesus said, "Come all who are weary and heavy laden." All means kings and lepers, beauty queens and wallflowers, athletes and benchwarmers. In God's eyes, there is no difference among them. All need his love.

Follow It Up

"Howard Grey," Ed Kilbourne
"Picture Perfect," Michael W. Smith

 # Authority Song

● ● ● ● ● ● ● ● ● ● ● ● ● ● ● ●

John Cougar Mellencamp (Mellencamp)
Uh-Huh
Riva Records
1983—*Reached number 15*

Crank It Up

In Mellencamp's earlier years, he cultivated a rebel image and even went by the created name, John Cougar. Through the chorus "I fight authority, authority, I always will," this song gives us a closer look at the younger John Cougar Mellencamp. We sense his need to question. People have changed their opinion of Mellencamp over the years, mostly because of his humanitarian efforts for the farmers, but he's still the same singer who once shook his fist at authority in every music video he appeared in. This rule-knocking song is vintage Mellencamp.

Talk It Up

- What rules did you hate when you were growing up?
- What rules do you dislike the most now? Why those?
- What kind of authority figures do you resist? What kinds most prompt your respect and cooperation?
- Why do people in authority often seem to let the power go to their heads?
- Are there some authorities you think are not even needed?
- How can you decide when you should resist authority and when you should obey?
- Are you ever in a position of authority? What kind of authority figure are you?

Look It Up

Romans 13:1–5. What kind of relationship should we have with our governmental authorities?

Matthew 21:12. What makes Jesus' action in this incident acceptable? How can we know the difference between situations we are to fight against and those we're not?

Romans 12:19–21. What action should we take against those who anger us? How do we conquer evil with good?

Wrap It Up

Most of us have no trouble picturing God as a wonderful Creator; nor do we struggle to see him as a benevolent superpower. Even the view of God as a loving father is a comforting image for many. But the image of God that most people find hardest to accept is the image of God as an authority figure.

The Bible presents a very clear picture of God as the authority. He is a king, a judge. Adam and Eve were expelled from the garden because of their sin. Moses was not allowed to enter the promised land because he disobeyed God. Someday all will stand before him to be judged. The difference between God and other authority figures is that God's rules and expectations do not change; they have been set for centuries. His demands are clear and fair. If we choose not to follow them, the blame is ours, not God's.

There are times God expects us to rise up and fight those who oppress us. God doesn't expect us to be doormats for others to walk on. Most of the time, however, God wants us to fight evil by doing good. The peace marches of the '60s are a good example of that principle in action. God wants us to learn the power of submission before entrusting us with the powerful office of leadership. Romans 12:21 says not to let evil get the upper hand; that implies an intentional monitoring on our part. The rest of the verse says to change evil by doing good; that requires that we monitor ourselves. Make things right by doing right. Use your displeasure with authority to effect positive change—rather than more displeasure.

Follow It Up

"Signs," Five Man Electrical Band*
"Take This Job and Shove It," Johnny Paycheck

 **Benediction**

• • • • • • • • • • •

Susan Ashton (Kirkpatrick and Simon)
Wakened by the Wind
Sparrow
1991

Crank It Up

This is a great song about moving on in our lives. Often the process of growing requires us to leave the familiar and comfortable and venture out into uncharted ground. To feel as though we are not abandoning our former commitment, we seek approval from those who have given us direction along the way. Like a child leaving for college, a bride being given away at her wedding, or even a young person receiving a job promotion from a proud supervisor, we relish the moment of starting off on our own with the blessing of those we respect and love.

Talk It Up

- What clubs, teams, or organizations have you been a part of in the past?
- What "good-byes" did you receive from them? a banquet? a diploma? something else?
- How do you say good-bye to people you love? Is it difficult for you?
- Will you soon be moving on to something new in your life? If so, what kind of "benediction" might make the transition easier or more meaningful?
- Have you felt God's benediction upon your life? If so, in what ways? If not, how might you gain a sense of his blessing?

Look It Up

Genesis 27. Why did Jacob go to such lengths to trick Esau? What did Isaac's blessing do for Jacob?

21

1 Chronicles 4:10. Why did Jabez ask God for his blessing?
Proverbs 10:22. What promises come with God's blessing?
Proverbs 28:20. What kind of people seek God's blessing?

Wrap It Up

Most church services end with a benediction. In traditional churches, the same blessing is pronounced week after week. Often, we barely hear the words as we prepare to move back out into the world, yet it may be the most important part of a service. A benediction invokes God's blessing upon us. Have you ever asked someone, "Wish me luck" as you prepare to embark on a new venture? A benediction is like having God wish you luck, only he is capable of doing much more than that.

Susan Ashton captures the need for benediction in our lives. In our spiritual journeys, we are constantly taking new paths, scaling new heights, or testing new waters. God's blessing is vital at all times. We should free benedictions from the confines of church tradition and experience them daily in our walk with the Lord. It is so much more effective than luck. Benedictions, while usually said at closings, are really blessings for beginnings.

Follow It Up

"Stay," Jackson Browne
"Make My Life a Prayer to You," Keith Green
"Who Am I," Margaret Becker

Boy Like Me/ Man Like You

● ● ● ● ● ● ● ● ● ● ● ● ●

Rich Mullins (Mullins and Beaker)
The World as Best as I Remember It, Vol. 1
Reunion Records
1991

Crank It Up

Many people wonder about the younger days of Jesus' life. What was he like as a child? How did he relate to other boys and girls? This song is an imaginative attempt to fill in the blanks around Jesus' childhood. With his usual flair, Rich sings about snow angels and laughing friends; he imagines what it would have been like to grow up with Jesus.

Talk It Up

- What do you imagine Jesus was like as a teenager? What kinds of things might he have gotten involved in? What kind of friends did he hang out with?
- What was your childhood like? How do you think it might have been similar to Jesus' childhood? How might it have been different?
- What would you like to know about Jesus' growing up days? How would that information affect you?
- Can any of us expect to be like Jesus? How old does one have to be to be like him?
- In what areas of your life do you still need to grow up?

Look It Up

1 Timothy 4:12. What things in your life are good examples for others to follow? Have you ever been held up as an exam-

ple for others? Do you ever look at younger people as examples to follow? Why or why not?

Luke 2:40–52. This account is all we know about Jesus' childhood. Are there other things you would like to know? What?
Why? What were you like at age twelve? How have you
changed?

1 Corinthians 11:1. Have you imitated Jesus in your life? What
do you need to work on?

Wrap It Up

Jesus' life has meant more to the history of the world and to
each one of us than any other event. He gives us salvation, a model
to follow in reaching out to others, and words of wisdom to shape
our lives. It is sometimes easy to forget that he was also a human.
He ate home cooking. He had blisters on his hands. He told jokes
and laughed hard when someone else did.

It would be interesting to know what Jesus' daily schedule was
like. If we could only watch his home movies or visit his third
grade class, we would be able to know him better. These details
would splash even more color into his vivid life and help us focus
on his human side.

Unfortunately, there is much that we don't know about Jesus'
life. God has kept some things secret, at least for now. This should
not lessen our desire to know him as Savior and Lord; it should
make us want to know him even more! We can be the color
splashes that fill in the details of Jesus' life. Our lives are reflec-
tions of his, no matter what age we are.

God's gift to us was not just a distant historical spirit. He was
a human being. God wants us to imitate his Son and offer our
lives to him. This will make boys and girls grow bold and men
and women walk straight.

Follow It Up

"Turning Thirty," Randy Stonehill*
"Forever Young," Rod Stewart*

 # Busy Man

● ● ● ● ● ● ● ● ● ●

Steven Curtis Chapman (Chapman)
For the Sake of the Call
Sparrow Records
1990

Crank It Up

In this song, Christian superstar Steven Curtis Chapman offers a reality check. The story in the song prompts us to reflect on what's important in life. We aren't graded on whose stack of stuff is bigger. God wants us to work on developing our souls, not our bank accounts. Too many of us are still confused.

Talk It Up

Pass out pencils and paper and ask the group to write out their typical weekday routines in half-hour intervals. Then discuss:

- What do you spend the most time on?
- What do you spend the least amount of time on?
- What areas of your life are most important to you? How much time do you spend pursuing or developing those areas?
- What would you like to spend more time on? less time on?
- What amount of time do you have no control over?
- What amount of time can you control?

Look It Up

Matthew 16:26. What are you trying to gain? What is the cost to you? How valuable is your soul to you?

Luke 10:38–41. Are you more like Mary or Martha? In what ways?

Mark 6:31. Why did Jesus want to take a break? What do you need to take a break from? Why?

Psalm 46:10. When did you last stop to enjoy God? How can you begin to do it more often?

Wrap It Up

Today's teenagers may be the busiest in history. Our society has convinced them that the busier they are, the more successful they will be. Their days are filled with soccer games, dance lessons, part-time jobs, piano lessons, drama rehearsals, and countless other activities. Many have been on the fast track since they took their first steps. An elementary school gym teacher commented in a newspaper article that for the first time in all her years of teaching, she had to teach her young students how to play tag because they had never played it before.

When we believe that the road to success is paved with activity after activity, we begin to think that doing is the same as being. We feel it is only after we *do* enough that we earn the right to *be*. The problem with this view is that when the activity ceases, we find that we don't like what we've become. Because we have not learned to relax, we have missed so much along the way. We don't know how to enjoy life.

We need to remind ourselves that God cares for us because of who we *are*, not what we *do*. He wants nothing from us other than our love. He wants us to love him with all that we have, all that we are. God wants us and us alone. Stop rushing about, look into his eyes, and enjoy.

Follow It Up

"Cat's in the Cradle," Harry Chapin
"Once You Understand," Think

Change in My Life

John Pagano (Straus)
Leap of Faith
MCA Records
1992

Crank It Up

This classic gospel song with an old-fashioned sound is a bright spot in the Steve Martin movie about a phony evangelist. Backed by a choir on the chorus, the song builds to a crescendo as the words "There's a change in my life since you came along," ring out. In the midst of a cynical screenplay, this song gives a glimpse of the true gospel message.

Talk It Up

- What's the worst day in your life you can remember? the best?
- When have you been lonely? cheated? misunderstood?
- Has your life changed at all since your decision to follow Christ?
- In what ways do you still need to let Jesus change you?

Look It Up

Mark 5:1–20. How did the man in this story change upon meeting Jesus? Do you think people noticed the difference? Why?
Mark 10:46–52. What kind of change was apparent in Bartimaeus's life? Do you think people noticed the difference?
Luke 19:1–9. How did meeting Jesus change Zacchaeus? Do you think people noticed the difference? Why?

Wrap It Up

It's exciting to hear new Christians talk about the change in their lives following a commitment to Christ. For some, the change is drastic: a life full of pain and sin is turned around completely to peace and contentment. With such individuals, the signs of change are often obvious. It may be a new attitude, new friends, or new values. For others, however, the change is harder to identify. The line of before Christ and after Christ is often blurred. For young people raised in the church, the line often appears to be nonexistent. Yet without a doubt, the presence of Christ will always change our lives.

We need to remember that the change is not a one-time thing. Even with a commitment to Christ, we still may be lonely, cheated, or misunderstood. We may still experience difficulty and depression; we will still endure failure and frustration. It is then that we call upon Christ, who because of our commitment is always present. He brings about the change again and again. The real change of becoming a Christian is not that your whole life goes from bad to good; it is that no matter how bad things get (and they may) and no matter how you mess up (and you will), Christ is there to change it to good. We have been saved by grace and Christ has assured our salvation. *That* will never change.

Follow It Up

"Man in the Mirror," Michael Jackson[*]
"Cool Change," Little River Band[*]

Charm Is Deceitful

Kim Hill (King and Hill)
Talk About Life
Reunion Records
1989

Crank It Up

The text of this song is based on Proverbs 31:30. Its message is simple and to the point: Women who work hard at being beautiful on the outside should also work at being beautiful on the inside. "Charm is deceitful and beauty is vain, but a woman who fears the Lord shall be praised," Kim sings. Her message is as timeless as the Word of God.

Talk It Up

- Who do you consider the most beautiful woman in the world? Do beautiful women get the most attention? If so, why do you think that's true?
- Why does our culture put so much emphasis on beauty and exercise?
- Do women sometimes use charm as a form of manipulation? Explain.
- Why is charm deceitful? Why is beauty vain? Do you know women who are beautiful because of their spiritual commitment?
- How can we get to the place where women who fear the Lord are praised? What might men have to change? What do women need to do?

Look It Up

Proverbs 31:10–31. How many beauty techniques can you list that women use to enhance their appearance? How many items from the list are mentioned in the Scripture passage?

Romans 10:15. What makes us truly beautiful (even down to our feet)? What actions should we begin to display if we desire true beauty?

Isaiah 52:7. What does God find beautiful?

Wrap It Up

People magazine once printed an article on the eating habits of three supermodels. The models spoke of eating minuscule amounts in order to maintain their model status. One model recalled crying after being criticized for eating lettuce. These women willingly abused their bodies to be "beautiful." In turn, the media touts these women as standards for beauty—standards that are unreachable for most women in our society. As a result, many women are persuaded that they are substandard.

We live in a society where looks are put at the top of the list. The cosmetic industry is worth billions. Food companies spend thousands on packaging alone. Automobile companies come out with new models every year. The truth is that packaging is relatively unimportant. It is what is on the inside that really counts.

The rise of generic food brands and generic drugs shows that some people recognize that slick packaging often misleads. We are now able to accept food in plain packages. Unfortunately, we are still a long way off from accepting people in plain packages.

The Bible gives more advice on developing inner beauty than outer beauty. Jesus tells us we shouldn't be overly concerned with our outward appearance (Matt. 6:25–34). Solomon reminds us that charm is deceitful and beauty is vain (Prov. 31:30). The Lord told Samuel that man may look on the outward appearance, but God sees the inner beauty of the heart (1 Sam. 16:7).

If we want to spend more time developing inner beauty, we are going to have to change the way we think about ourselves. We must learn to view ourselves as hearts and minds to nurture, not bodies to craft. We must begin to see ourselves as God sees us. As we begin to place more importance on what we look like on the inside, we will stop caring that we are not perfect on the outside. God will honor our sincere efforts to please him, and we will begin to develop a true beauty that will never fade away.

Follow It Up

"Picture Perfect," Michael W. Smith
"You're So Vain," Carly Simon

 # Christmas Time

● ● ● ● ● ● ● ● ● ● ● ● ● ● ●

Larry Norman (Norman)
So Long Ago the Garden
Phydeauz Records Bone
1980

Crank It Up

Christmas is the time of the year when we want to just sit back and enjoy the season. We try to get all the shopping done early so we won't panic as the big day approaches. However, it never happens like we want it to. Our malls are full right up to the last minute and our roads are jammed full with cars whose horns all work. Shopping lists are scrutinized over and over for fear of leaving someone out. We cover our bases furiously as we go from our office parties to every family gathering imaginable. What was begun as a quiet celebration has over the years picked up steam and now has a two-month life of its own. This song is about our favorite season and how we've given it a bad name.

Talk It Up

- What was your favorite Christmas ever? What were your favorite presents?
- What family customs do you observe during Christmas time?
- Do you think Christmas is too commercial? What ways would you change it? What parts of the season would you emphasize?
- How far ahead do you start buying Christmas gifts? Do you enjoy the special sales and seasonal trappings?
- Does your celebration of Christmas reflect the true meaning of Christmas? How?

Look It Up

Matthew 1:18–2:12. Read the Christmas story. Create a new celebration of Christ's birth based solely on the Scriptures.

31

What parts should be highlighted? What parts have been exaggerated? Make a contract for your family to sign that stresses a new outlook on Christmas. Include specifics on how much time to spend on activities that promote the real meaning of Christmas, how much time to spend with relatives, how much time to devote to actions done for the good of others.

Wrap It Up

To children, Christmas is the most magical time of the year. Every tradition, every decoration, and every song lights up their young faces. Christmas is experienced with wonder and awe.

As we get older, our view of Christmas often changes. Suddenly the traditions seem forced. The decorations appear plastic and the songs ring false. The magic is gone. We blame it on the commercialization of Christmas and our ignorance as children.

However, if we take a closer look, the things that make Christmas magical are still there. The reason for the holiday hasn't changed; what has changed is us. We have forgotten to look past the plastic and commercials to the magic of a baby being born.

Christmas still celebrates the birth of our Lord and Savior. It still has the ability to touch people in a way they never feel any other time of the year. More people attend church at Christmas than any other time of the year. It is up to us to continue to celebrate the miraculous birth of our Savior with reverence and awe. We need to emphasize the magic of the traditions, the beauty of the decorations, and the joy of the songs. If we do this, perhaps more people will follow us to the manger.

Follow It Up

Traditional Christmas carols
"Gimme, Gimme, Gimme," Haupert and Smith

 # Church

• • • • • • •

Lyle Lovett (Lovett)
Joshua Judges Ruth
MCA/Curb
1992

Crank It Up

Lyle Lovett has a knack for looking at things in an unusual way. His bizarre story of a church service that goes on and on is also a humorous account of a miracle—the miracle that comes from asking for the common and receiving the extraordinary.

Talk It Up

- What's the strangest thing you've ever seen in a church service?
- What do you think is the point of Lyle Lovett's song?
- Does your pastor and church staff keep your interest in Sunday services? If so, how? If not, how could they do so?
- What kinds of things do you wish you could see more of in church?
- If you were creating your church's worship service this Sunday, how would you change it?

Look It Up

Acts 2:42–47. What ingredients were part of the typical first century church service? What were the results? How does that pattern (and results) compare to your church's worship services?

Acts 19:1–7. How do you think the early church differed from your church? How was it the same?

Acts 20:7–12. Has anyone in your church ever been bored to death? Apparently that's what happened to Eutychus! What things does the church gathering described in these verses have in common with your church?

Wrap It Up

Complaining about church services is a time-tested Christian ritual—the service is too long, the sermons are boring, the music is too slow, the sanctuary lighting is poor. The list goes on and on. But is it the church's duty to entertain us? Nowhere in the Bible does it command pastors to create worship services for our pleasure. On the contrary, the worship service is for God's pleasure. The word *worship* is derived from *worthship*, which means God is worthy of our praise. We ought to go to church for his benefit, not ours.

We need to get back to the basics of worship. We need to stop making excuses and worship God in his house every Sunday. We need to get involved and actively participate in the service. Finally, we need to fill the service with joy and thanksgiving, for God is worthy of our praise.

Follow It Up

"Mississippi Squirrel Revival," Ray Stevens
"Back Row Sanctuary Blues," Ed Kilbourne

 # Closer to Fine

• • • • • • • • • • • • • •

Indigo Girls (Saliers)
Indigo Girls
Epic Records
1989—*Reached number 52*

Crank It Up

Most Indigo Girls tunes are extremely layered and full of tangents to follow; this song is no exception. It is about how to approach life and its questions. The title of the song is their answer to the question, Am I headed in the right direction with my life? From friends to teachers to even the church, they looked for meaning to life and eventually discovered the less they worry about it, the better off they feel. This seems a very shallow response to the deep question but in its simpleness, it answers with a delicate clearness.

Talk It Up

- What question would you like to ask God when you see him? What do you think he will say? What might he ask you when he sees you?
- What do you think the Indigo Girls mean by the phrase, "closer to fine"? What might they mean when they sing, "The less I seek my source for some definitive, the closer I am to fine"?
- Do you ever wonder about the purpose of life? What is your reason for living? Do you think it's important to know?

Look It Up

Philippians 1:6. What do you think this verse means? What does it say about your present? your future?
Romans 8:28. What is God's purpose for us?
Ephesians 1:12. How do we thank him?

Wrap It Up

We live in a society where no matter what the question is, somebody has an answer for it. Seldom are these answers put forth as theory, but rather as truth. We have been quick to accept answers in spite of a lack of evidence. So we've gone through life wearing our earth shoes and crystals, taking our megavitamins, and plotting our biorhythms. As each answer fails to answer our questions, we turn to the next one.

It is amazing that we continue to embrace the current popular "truth." It is even more incredible when we realize we have had the correct answer all along. There is only one answer or truth that has not changed with the whims of popular culture. It has remained constant in spite of attempts to prove or disprove it. It is one answer that few people turn away from once they accept it. It is God's truth. Only God's truth remains the same as it was when he first gave it through his Son. Only God's truth fits even when popular culture changes. Only God's truth holds meaning for each individual's circumstances.

Many people criticize Christians for believing in an answer without concrete evidence. The response should be as the Indigo Girls put it: It's better to be on the path to perfection, to be closer to fine, than to be sitting around waiting for another wrong truth. We do well to admit that we haven't arrived yet; we don't have all the answers. We should simply rest in the fact that we are still under construction. The "crooked lines" alluded to in the song that offer many different answers don't always need our approval or even our scrutiny. We can let God be God and stay committed to him, knowing that he has a purpose for us. Seek God's face and you will also be closer to fine.

Follow It Up

"On the Road to Find Out," Cat Stevens
"Eagle Song," The Imperials

 # Color Blind

● ● ● ● ● ● ● ● ● ●

Michael W. Smith (Smith, Kirkpatrick,
    and Huff)
Change Your World
Reunion Records
1992

Crank It Up

Michael W. Smith challenges us to get past our differences of
color and look at each other as equals. Each new generation
parades its openness and claims the end to racism. But companies still practice discriminatory hiring practices, race riots still
break out in American cities, and people still judge other people
on the basis of skin color. His question, "Why can't we be color
blind?" is one we continue to ask.

Talk It Up

- How many ethnic groups can you name? What characteristics or stereotypes do people apply unfairly to each group?
- Do you have any close relationships with people of a different ethnic group?
- How can you help yourself and others to become color
  blind?

Look It Up

2 Kings 17:24–41. Who made up the people of Samaria? What
    was their crime that persisted over centuries?
John 4:1–26. What prejudicial act did the woman encounter
    regularly? What promise did Jesus make to her?
Acts 8:4–8. What happened when Philip loved the Samaritans
    enough to preach the gospel in their midst?
Galatians 3:26–29. How do these verses apply to today's racial
    distinctions and differences?

Wrap It Up

Racism, prejudice, and ignorance are woven into the fabric of our daily lives, poisoning our relationships and our communities. Tragically, even God's Word has been used at times to justify racism and hatred. But Jesus made it clear that such conduct is anti-Christian. In three separate accounts in the New Testament, Jesus used the people of Samaria to spread his message of God's love. They were no different in his eyes than any other group.

The core of the gospel is the command to "love your neighbor as yourself" (Mark 12:33). When we love others as we love ourselves, there is no difference between us. It means we recognize the person, not the skin color or culture. A child of God is a child of God, and a true follower of Christ is color blind.

Follow It Up

"The Great American Novel," Larry Norman[*]
"Black or White," Michael Jackson

Coming Out of the Dark

Gloria Estefan (Estefan, Estefan Jr., and Secada)
Into the Light
Epic Records
1991—*Reached number 1*

Crank It Up

In 1990, at what seemed the height of her career, Gloria Estefan was involved in a near-fatal car crash. This beautiful song is the result of much soul-searching during her long and painful recovery. The words of this song, written by Gloria's husband, depict their love for each other with deeply spiritual overtones. "Coming out of the dark, I finally see the light now," she sings, concluding with, "Forever I'll stand on the rock."

Talk It Up

- Where is the darkest place you've ever been? A cave? a darkroom? somewhere else? How does it feel to be in a completely dark place?
- When was the darkest period of your life? How hard was it to start back to recovery? Did anyone help you along the way?
- Did God play a role in getting you out? What role would you have liked him to play?
- What things do you think God can do for you in times of trouble and trial? Does he ever use other people?

Look It Up

James 1:1–5. What purpose does trouble play in our lives? How does God let us know we are growing through troubles?
Ephesians 4:18. What are some reasons for being in darkness?
Psalm 112:4. Who receives the light? Why does God give us help? What does he expect?

Wrap It Up

Darkness. From the time you were small, it has been an element to be feared. We use night-lights in our children's bedrooms. The first thing we do when we enter a room is turn on a light. The majority of people, if given a choice, would choose light over darkness. Darkness means unknown and the unknown is scary. Light gives the ability to see clearly. What we see and understand we seldom fear.

In the literal sense, darkness and light are easy to identify and understand. In the theological sense, they are a bit more difficult to define. The Bible defines darkness as walking without God. We have light when our lives are illuminated through a relationship with Christ. The difficult part is that it is often hard to see the darkness we are walking in. Since it is not a physical darkness, it is easy to delude ourselves into thinking that we are not experiencing darkness.

Gloria Estefan's darkness was the result of a car accident that gravely injured her. Her husband wrote this song to describe his feelings as he moved through recovery with her. First, there was darkness as her life hung in the balance. Then there was gradual light as it became apparent that she would survive. For Gloria, the darkness during this time was literal—she was unconscious. A different kind of darkness remained after she regained consciousness. Her days were spent in a haze of pain. She was unable to see beyond her tragedy. The light finally came as she was able to move beyond herself and out into the world.

For many of us, our darkness is similar. Because of sin or our particular circumstances, our days are spent concerned only about ourselves. When our eyes are on ourselves, we lose all perspective. We become calloused, hardened, and bitter. We need light to be able to see clearly again.

Nothing makes less sense than wandering around in the dark. If someone were stumbling around in a dark room searching for something, we would probably shout, "Turn on the light!" Come out of the dark and into the Light. Light with a capital L. The Light that is of God. For only then can we see clearly and leave our painful selves behind.

Follow It Up

"Slow Train Coming," Bob Dylan

 # Cool Change

• • • • • • • • • • • • •

Little River Band (Shorrock)
First under the Wire
Capitol Records
1979—*Reached number 10*

Crank It Up

Every once in awhile our lives get so overloaded with activity we need to get away and relax. Even more than just relaxing, we need to rearrange our lives to recover a sense of balance. This song points to the beneficial effects of rest and solitude. We take care of ourselves by taking time alone to recharge our energies. "Cool change" is a challenge to do just that more often.

Talk It Up

- Where is your favorite place to think?
- What kinds of things cause you stress?
- What things do you enjoy doing for yourself to get away from the pressure? How often do you do them?
- Who among your friends can tell when you are out of sorts and in need of a change?
- What changes can you make in your life to ensure a "cool change" every now and then? What would these changes do to the outlook you have on your life?

Look It Up

Matthew 14:22–23. Why do you think Jesus felt the need to be alone? Was it physical? emotional? spiritual?
Luke 9:18. What do you think Luke means by saying Jesus "was alone and his disciples were with him" (KJV)? Have you ever been alone when others were around?
John 6:14–15. Did Jesus retreat because he was afraid? If not, why did he retreat?

Psalm 37:7. Is there a difference between resting and resting in
the Lord?

Wrap It Up

Every youth group or high school class has had one: a kid who
is so dynamic that his presence ignites the entire group, a kid
who is so tireless and devoted to the group that he seems des-
tined for greatness, a kid who, after a few years, fizzles and fades
away altogether. Group members find themselves asking, "What
happened?" More often than not, the problem is burnout.

The human body—and even spirit—is like a supercharged race
car. The car can go at phenomenal speeds, performing superbly.
Yet in a single race, a driver will stop as many as twenty times to
recharge the car. It needs more fuel, new tires, and several adjust-
ments in order to keep going at such speeds. Like that car, we are
capable of tremendous action, but we can't keep going without
frequent stops to recharge and refuel. It is a lesson that is taught
throughout the Bible. Jesus continually took time to retreat and
spend time with God before continuing with his ministry. The
very last thing he did before facing trial and crucifixion was to
spend time in prayer with God. Paul, too, relied heavily on the
prayers and encouragement of the churches he helped start. The
road was simply too long and the task was too great not to do so.

God calls us to be people of action, moving throughout the
world to do his will. But he does not expect us to do it ourselves.
In fact, he expects us to draw upon his power. Tapping into that
power may require an abrupt change. It may mean slowing, or
even stopping for a time. It may mean retreating instead of
advancing. Such cool changes, however, keep us in the race.

Follow It Up

"Sailing," Christopher Cross
"Just Come In," Margaret Becker

Cosmetic Fixation

Randy Stonehill (Stonehill)
Equator
Myrrh
1983

Crank It Up

This is a song about our fixation on always looking good. We will try and do almost anything to keep our image perfect. The four billion dollars we spend on cosmetics each year will soon double as we buy into the lie that "what you see is what you get." Our hair, our face, and our fingernails are all part of our earth suit that gets more than its share of attention. Randy Stonehill sings of how ridiculous it is to put so much time and energy into something that is so unimportant.

Talk It Up

- What is your morning "get ready to go" procedure?
- What part of your body (if any) would you alter if you could? How?
- How much money do you spend on your appearance in a month? Is it worth it?
- How does the way you look affect the way you act?
- Do you think there's too much emphasis placed on looks in our society? Why?
- What would people think about you if you didn't work so hard at how you look?
- What would it cost to put more time and energy into keeping your "insides" in shape? Why don't more people work harder on their personalities?

Look It Up

1 Peter 3:3–4. What kind of beauty does God value? How can we get it?

Matthew 6:25–34. What do these verses tell us about how concerned we should be with our appearance? What should we do instead?

Wrap It Up

It was once said, "Half the work that is done in this world is to make things appear what they are not." Cosmetic companies would probably agree and even applaud that statement. They would explain that there is nothing wrong with looking our best. They would say that looking our best does wonders for our self-confidence. They would assert that only when we are feeling confident can we accomplish our goals and achieve success.

But looking good will never heal or build up our inner self. It is just a quick fix on the surface. It's like putting beautiful, expensive wallpaper over a bumpy, pitted wall. It may look quite good at first, but eventually the wall's defects will show through the paper. The paper will wrinkle and sag over the holes. In time, the paper will lose its beauty and reflect only what is wrong with the underlying wall.

Jesus came to save our souls, not our bodies. Yet we spend more time on our physical bodies than our spiritual health. Though society's standard of outward beauty is constantly changing, God's standard for inner beauty remains the same. We need to learn to swing the balance in the other direction. Your appearance tells the world who you are on the surface; your soul tells people who you are underneath—a child of God.

Follow It Up

"Picture Perfect," Michael W. Smith
"Vogue," Madonna

Defenders of the Flag

Bruce Hornsby and The Range (Hornsby and Hornsby)
Scenes from the Southside
RCA Records
1988

Crank It Up

Every day, it seems, our newspapers have a story about a political leader gone bad, a priest and his dark side, a trusted executive who stole from his company. It has become so common that our shock and outrage have worn thin and we have come to expect the worst of our leaders. Our "defenders of the flag" are taking bribes on the side, making deals in back rooms, and falling from grace in our public arenas. Hornsby sings, "If these guys are the good ones, I don't want to know the bad."

Talk It Up

- Who is your favorite president of all time? least favorite?
- How involved are you in student government at your school?
- Do you know of any misdealings by trusted leaders? How does it make you feel when these become public?
- Would you ever want to be a politician? How would you be different from the rest? How would you be the same?

Look It Up

2 Peter 2:3–22. Compare the false teachers mentioned in this passage to today's political leaders. How are they similar? How are they different?

Romans 13:1–5. How does this passage apply to us today? Does it apply to leaders you didn't vote for? corrupt leaders? oppressive leaders?

Wrap It Up

In the '70s, Robert Redford starred in a movie called *The Candidate*. He played an idealistic young man who is encouraged to run for office. He entered the political race convinced he could make a difference for all the right reasons. Yet he slid into the dirty world of political gain and compromise, eventually sinking so low that he punches a constituent in the face.

In 1993, another movie was made in which a look-alike is used as a stand-in for a sick president. The movie *Dave* shows how the look-alike's honesty and sincerity completely changed an administration previously run by greed and corruption.

Which is more accurate, *The Candidate* or *Dave*? Is it possible to create governing bodies based on truth rather than deceit or power? Most people would probably say that the task is too difficult. Many feel that the average American has little to say in government. However, the constitution has not been overturned or rewritten. The same ideals our founding fathers wrote—based on Christian tenets—are still the foundation of our government.

The average American must take a stand. We must quit financing campaigns of those who misuse their elected power. We must demand morality from our elected officials. We must let candidates know that dirty campaigns will cost votes. We must convince our friends and neighbors that voting is a powerful weapon. America has been given much in terms of material wealth and personal freedom. As a nation, she must show she is worthy of it.

Follow It Up

"American Pie," Don McLean
"The End of the Innocence," Don Henley[*]

◻️ Disease of Conceit

• • • • • • • • • • • • • • • • • • •

Bob Dylan (Dylan)
Oh Mercy
Columbia Records
1989

Crank It Up

Conceit is to think more highly of ourselves than we should. This song warns us of the dangers of conceit. It can make us believe things about ourselves and others that aren't always true. The English poet Alexander Pope said, "Conceit is to nature what paint is to beauty; it is not only needless, but it impairs what it would improve."

Talk It Up

- Do you know anyone who is conceited? Describe that person. How does that person make you feel?
- Are you ever guilty of conceit? Why is it so easy to notice conceit in others and so difficult to see it in ourselves?
- How does conceit affect us? What does it make us do?
- What's the difference between conceit and self-confidence?

Look It Up

Romans 12:16. How does this verse command us to act? Can you think of examples of that kind of conduct?

Proverbs 28:11. Can money make us conceited? How? What is noticeable to the poor that the rich don't see?

Proverbs 26:4, 5. How should we talk with conceited people? What will this accomplish?

Philippians 2:3–8. How can we reflect the mind of Christ? What specifics can we start working on today to do that?

Wrap It Up

One of the greatest difficulties humans face is to maintain an accurate picture of themselves. People often see themselves very differently from the way others see them. Usually, their self-image falls short of the image they project to others. Parents, teachers, ministers, and psychologists devote a lot of time to the building of self-esteem. A strong self-esteem is essential to reaching our potential as human beings.

Sometimes, however, our self-image becomes inflated, and we begin to view ourselves as better than others. That view then directly affects all of our relationships.

Conceit turns a person inward. All thoughts and actions are based on how they will affect the self. A person who is turned inward is incapable of reaching out to people, and is often unable to see his or her sin.

Christians are not immune to conceit. We are often quick to pat ourselves on the back for having found the right answer and for doing the right things. We build churches and denominations on our goodness. We slowly begin to turn inward, glorifying our goodness. We even begin to become intolerant of those who can't measure up. In short, we become infected with the disease of conceit.

The apostle Paul continually talks of his struggles. In each letter to the various churches, he reminds them of his faults and he offers thanks for their assistance. Paul knew that he had to avoid the disease of conceit. He did this in two ways. First, he openly acknowledged his faults and struggles. Second, he reached out to others.

We must follow his example and stop the spread of this disease by admitting our faults and reaching out to others. Be willing to always think of others before you think of yourself.

Follow It Up

"You're So Vain," Carly Simon
"Charm Is Deceitful," Kim Hill*

Don't Tell Them Jesus Loves Them (Until You're Ready to Love Them Too)

Steve Camp (Camp and Frazier)
Justice
Sparrow Records
1989

Crank It Up

Our television channels are full of well-dressed preachers reading the Bible to us from carpeted stages thousands of miles away. The only contact we have with these spiritual well-wishers, outside of the tube, is the monthly tithing envelopes we send them. Steve Camp sings about a much different style of reaching people—the method Jesus employed. When our words are backed up with our actions, the results are much more effective and lasting. This song exhorts us to not only speak the truth, but to live it as well.

Talk It Up

- How many people do you see or talk to daily? Make a list.
- How many of these people are Christians?
- Which of these people know you are a Christian? How do they know?
- Who do you talk to about Christ? Why those people?
- What kinds of people do you find it difficult to be around?
- What do you need to know about a person before you share Christ with them?
- How do you feel when someone you don't know begins asking spiritual questions of you? How do you respond?
- Who gives you spiritual advice?

Look It Up

> *John 4:1–30.* Why was the woman surprised that Jesus asked her for a drink of water? Do you think she was open or defensive in her conversation with Jesus? Why? Did Jesus condemn her for her living arrangements? Why not? How did he show her love? How did that make a difference in the presentation of the gospel?

Wrap It Up

Spreading the gospel. Evangelizing. Witnessing. We have numerous names for it. And we have numerous reasons why we don't do it. We are afraid of offending someone; we haven't been called by God; we are afraid of what people will think; we are just plain afraid. Yet we are called to spread the news of Jesus Christ to the world. So we gather our courage and head out to do the Lord's work, armed with reference Bibles, tracts, testimonies, and sinners' prayers. Often, we are left standing in wonder as they turn away from us. We might even believe that they were too deep in their sin to hear us. Were they? Maybe they did hear us; maybe that's the trouble.

What this song is telling us is that we cannot share the love of Christ with someone without loving them first. It is easy for Christians to pat themselves on the back for living good and moral lives. We tend to get a bit smug. We have the answers. We're doing things the right way. It is now up to us to save those poor, lost souls. We may not say such things out loud, but we express it loud and clear through our body language and our choice of words. Jesus had the unique ability to look deep into people and see their souls. He could feel their hurts and fears. He understood them because he truly loved them. They were not souls to be saved, but people to be loved.

We must take the time to know and love people. We must learn to see them as Jesus sees them. We must show them the love that is only possible through Christ. We are not called to simply speak the gospel; we are called to share it. Don't tell others that Jesus loves them . . . *show* them. Let them see him in your actions and they will surely hear him in your words.

Follow It Up

"Thank You," Ray Boltz*

Down on My Knees

● ●

Susan Ashton (Kirkland)
Wakened by the Wind
Sparrow Records
1991

Crank It Up

What happens to the soul when it is confronted with tempta-tion? What effects does sin have on the heart? This song is about repentance, and how we are affected by our own imperfection. Susan Ashton sings about "going down on my knees" in humil-ity and seeking forgiveness. She sings from what may be an all-too-familiar list of sins and describes the condition sin puts us in.

Talk It Up

- What is the worst thing you have ever done? the meanest? most painful?
- In what ways do you show remorse or regret? Have you ever prayed for forgiveness on your knees? Why is that so often a position of repentance?
- For what sins do you need to be forgiven? Why don't we confess more often?
- How would you describe the feeling after you "stand back up" (after you have been forgiven)?

Look It Up

James 4:17; Romans 14:23; 1 John 3:4. What is sin (according to these verses)? Can you give examples of each type of sin?
Hebrews 10:26; 1 Corinthians 6:9; Romans 6:23. What are sin's consequences (according to these verses)? What immediate consequences do we feel here on earth?
1 John 1:9. What is the solution for sin? How do we do that?

Wrap It Up

Most today tend to view the concept of sin in one of two ways. Many don't believe sin is a problem for them because they don't do anything *that* bad. They equate sin with the "big wrongs" such as murder, robbery, or rape. But sin is sin, whether it is grand larceny or petty thievery. As James 4:17 says, even when we fail to do good, we sin.

Others, however, go overboard in their view of their sin. They feel so overwhelmed by the weight of their sin, they think that redemption is out of the question. They doubt that God could ever forgive what they have done. But 1 John 1:9 promises that if we confess our sins, God will forgive us and cleanse us from our sins.

Susan Ashton's song is for all of us. No one is perfect; all have sinned. When we "go down" on our knees, God will forgive us and wipe our slate clean.

Follow It Up

"I Am a Servant," Larry Norman*
"Soften Your Heart," Keith Green

 Dust in the Wind

• • • • • • • • • • • • • • • • • •

Kansas (Livgren)
Point of Know Return
Kirshner Records
1977—Reached number 6

Crank It Up

The '70s supergroup Kansas was known for mixing classical music styles with mainstream rock to achieve a sound unlike that of any other group. They have always prided themselves in crafting honest lyrics with their classic melodies. This song talks about the fleetingness of life; we are all going to return to the earth as dust. Many people in our society use this as an excuse for grabbing all the gusto they can while they are still alive. We need to give people God's side of the story.

Talk It Up

- Have you ever been struck by the fragility of life? If so, what were the circumstances that made you feel that way?
- If you knew you would die next week, would you do anything differently than you've done this past week?
- Do you know people who try to grab all they can get out of life without regard to their future?
- What things about our world depress you?
- If you knew the world would end tomorrow, who would you most want to talk to or spend time with? Why?

Look It Up

John 5:24–30. What awaits us after death? How does this affect your lifestyle now?

Luke 16:19–31. What would need to happen for us to be convinced our lives are important? Who would you like to talk to that has already died?

Ephesians 3:10, 11. For what purpose were we created? What specific purpose do you feel God has for you?

Psalm 103:13–18. Do the psalmist's words scare you or comfort you? Why?

Wrap It Up

Because this song is so depressing, it is actually surprising that it became such a hit. It compares humans to a piece of dirt that can be blown away by the wind. While it is a bit extreme, most people would probably agree that they will leave no more impact on the world than a piece of dirt. Because they feel so unimportant, many people live their lives with no hope for the future, no concern for others, and no reason to even exist.

The hope of the gospel, which literally means "good news," was very good news to the people of Jesus' time. Although they recognized that they would someday return to dust, they struggled to live righteous lives in the present. The news of salvation gave them hope for their future. It also gave them purpose for their lives on earth—to spread the gospel.

Today is no different than two thousand years ago. People are sinking fast. Their minds cause them to believe there is no future, no purpose in life, but their hearts won't accept it. They need to be told the truth. They need to be given hope. We must remind them of the purpose that God has created us for. We are to live righteous lives and make it our goal to please him. Dust in the wind? Hardly.

Follow It Up

"Pine Box," Rossington Collins Band[*]

The End of the Innocence

Don Henley (Henley and Hornsby)
The End of the Innocence
Geffen Records
1989—*Reached number 8*

Crank It Up

"The End of the Innocence" is about what happens to us as we grow up. The things that are only known by older people somehow make their way down to us. We find out that not everyone is nice, cars are not made to last, and we will have to vote for the lesser of two evils sometimes. This eye-opening time can damage our outlook on life. We often adopt a "nobody-cares-so-I-won't-either" attitude, which will only make things worse.

Talk It Up

- What is your fondest childhood memory? What was your favorite day?
- When did you quit believing in Santa Claus? the tooth fairy? the Easter bunny? What happened the next time you celebrated the holiday? Did you reveal your new knowledge to others?
- What innocence is the song referring to? What do you think is the message of the song? What things would you rather not know much about?
- What do you think it means to "offer up your best defense"?

Look It Up

1 Corinthians 13:11. What does Paul mean by "putting childish things away"? Have you put away any childish things?
Mark 10:13–15. What does it mean to come to God as a little child?

1 Timothy 4:12. What lessons can be taught only by the young and innocent?

Wrap It Up

One of the saddest times in a parent's life is the day their child quits believing in the world of make-believe. The moment a child renounces Santa Claus is the moment the child embarks on the journey to adulthood. Suddenly, the child casts a cynical eye on the world and "figures" everything out. Real life is nothing like storybook life. It is full of pain and disappointment. Evil and corruption abound. We leave childhood behind when we take off the rose-colored glasses and view life clearly.

However, there are adults among us who have managed to maintain some of that childlike innocence. They can still see flowers amongst the thorns. Their magical view of the world comforts us. They are not ignorant of evil; they simply look past the evil to find the good. It is not a unique ability. It is a gift God has given to each and every one of his children.

God is aware that sin has invaded the world. But he wants us to find the joy in spite of the evil. He wants us to find pleasure in the simplest things. He wants us to be in awe of his creation. He wants us to remember that the world was meant to be good; he wants us to actively seek the good out and enjoy it.

We need not leave childlike ways behind as we grow older. God never asked us to give up our sense of innocent joy and childlike wonder. We can put away childish things while remaining childlike. If we do that, we can fully experience the kingdom of God. The innocence need only end if we let it.

Follow It Up

"Twenty Years Ago," Kenny Rogers*
"This Is the Land of Confusion," Genesis

 # Everybody Hurts

• • • • • • • • • • • • • • • •

R.E.M. (Berry, Buck, Mills, and Stipe)
Automatic for the People
Warner Bros. Records
1992—*Reached number 18*

Crank It Up

R.E.M. is known for deeply moving, emotional songs. This song is exactly that. "Everybody Hurts" is about the pain we feel in our lives. All of us are touched by the hurt of living in a fallen world; no one is exempt from pain or problems. As the Bible says, "[God] sends rain on the just and on the unjust" (Matt. 5:45). Everybody hurts means just that . . . everybody. If you can show the video with this song, it would be even more touching.

Talk It Up

- What's the worst physical pain you've ever felt? emotional pain?
- Who is the person who has helped you through pain the most often?
- How does pain affect you?
- Have you learned any techniques for dealing with pain? What are they?
- What people around you are hurting? How can you help them?

Look It Up

Psalm 55:1–8. David gives expression to his pain in this psalm. In what ways is he hurting?
Psalm 55:22. What advice does David give for handling pain?
Matthew 11:28, 29. Who is speaking in these verses? What promises does he make?

James 1:2–4. What good can come from pain? How may it benefit us?

Wrap It Up

One of the most isolating feelings we experience is pain. When we are happy, we can't wait to tell someone. When we are angry, we are usually angry at someone. It is when we hurt that we hurt alone. Pain (whether physical or emotional) turns us inward; we feel as though no one can understand our hurt. But isolation only increases the hurt. Many have sought the help of support groups to combat the destructiveness of isolation. Just about every disease, every psychological disorder, and every tragic event has a support group designed to help its victims. These groups do not claim to cure the disease or erase the tragedy. They do not offer solutions. Their purpose is to offer support and provide a place for the pain to be shared.

These groups work for several reasons. The first is that they enable people to dispel the myth that they are alone. The song is right . . . everybody hurts. There is a strong chance that somebody has experienced the very hurt you are feeling. Just to know you are not alone helps to ease the pain.

Another reason the groups work is that as you begin to share your pain, you release its grip on you. It is as if by keeping silent, the pain is locked inside. As you speak of your hurt and fears, you let them go.

Finally, the support groups ease your pain by allowing you to take your thoughts off yourself by supporting someone else through their pain.

Ultimately, however, most pain will only be healed when we take it to God our Comforter. He understands our pain. He sent his Son to endure pain on the cross for us. Because God—through his Son, Jesus Christ—is no stranger to pain, he is able to make our pain more bearable. We need to reach into his hand like a little child and let him walk us through the depths of despair. He will not necessarily deliver us from all pain, but he will help us to endure.

Follow It Up

"Pressure," Billy Joel[*]
"Hand to Hold On To," John Cougar Mellencamp

(Everything I Do) I Do It for You

Bryan Adams (Adams, Lange, and Kamen)
Waking Up the Neighbours
A&M Records
1991—*Reached number 1*

Crank It Up

This song, from the score to the movie *Robin Hood, Prince of Thieves*, was intended as a love song from Robin to Maid Marian. However, it might just as well describe the love God feels for us. When Adams sings, "I would die for you," he clearly describes the kind of love God has demonstrated for each of us.

Talk It Up

- Who was your first love? How did you let him or her know your feelings? What kinds of things did you do together?
- How many relationships have you had since? How many were wonderful?
- What kinds of ways do people let you know they care about you? What ways would you prefer?
- What would be the perfect relationship for you?
- How often do you intentionally sacrifice for other people? What are some ways you have?

Look It Up

Song of Solomon 4:1–16. The Song of Solomon is an ancient love poem. Does this part of the Bible surprise you in any way? Does it embarrass you? Why or why not? Why do you think such poetry might be in the Bible?

John 15:9–18. What does God expect from us when we love
others? How do you put your love in action?

Ephesians 3:17–21. How much does God love us? How can you
be filled up with God? How much do you love God? To what
length would you go to show him that love?

Wrap It Up

The romance industry thrives on the notion that true love waits
for everyone. They perpetuate the belief that somewhere out there
is an ideal love for each and every one of us, a love who lives solely
for the purpose of uplifting and encouraging us. It's a nice thought,
but reality often falls far short.

We humans find it difficult to act solely for the benefit of
another. Even when we fall in love, we possess a set of expectations or conditions the other person must meet to satisfy our
needs. As relationships fail, we are quick to blame the other person for not loving deeply enough. We simply do not realize our
own failings when it comes to lasting love. So many of us move
from relationship to relationship, looking for that deep selfless
love.

The romance writers are not entirely wrong, however. The sort
of love relationship they glorify does exist. But it is not a sexual
relationship. True, selfless, sacrificial love is from God. He is the
one who is able to put it into practice perfectly. He loves us deeply
in spite of our failings. He created the world to please us. He gave
up control to give us free choice even though he knew it would
result in our destruction. And he sent his Son to die for us in order
to free us from destruction. That is the type of love we seek.

When we have God's perfect love in our lives, then—and only
then—can we give that love to someone else.

Follow It Up

"Make My Life a Prayer to You," Keith Green
"I Am a Servant," Larry Norman*

 # Father and Son

• • • • • • • • • • • • • •

Cat Stevens (Stevens)
Tea for the Tillerman
A&M Records
1971

Crank It Up

This song is a dialogue between a father and his son. The father begins by giving his son some parental advice. Urging him to slow down and spend time on important matters, the father wants his son to learn from his dad's experience.

The son answers that his father really doesn't know him at all. He tells his father that "from the moment I could talk I was ordered to listen." The son expresses a strong desire to get away and live his own life.

The song goes back and forth between the two until the two are singing simultaneously. They never connect. The father remains oblivious to his son's frustration; the son remains unappreciative of his father's advice.

Talk It Up

- How would you state the father's viewpoint? the son's viewpoint?
- Why do you think there is such a gap between them?
- Does the father need to change? If so, how? Does the son need to change? If so, how?
- Have you ever had trouble communicating with your parents? Can the "generation gap" be closed? How?

Look It Up

Ephesians 6:1–4. What does it mean to honor your father and
   mother? How could someone tell if you were doing this?

1 Timothy 5:1–2. Why is it good to speak kindly and respect-
fully to those who are older than you? Why do some young
people speak harshly to older people?

1 Timothy 4:12. Do your parents or other adults look down on
you because of your youth? If so, how do you respond? Is
there a better way to respond?

Wrap It Up

God created the family to be a place where relationships are
strong and supportive, a place where children could learn and
grow while being protected from harm. God intended the par-
ent/child relationship to be a two-way street. Children should
honor their father and mother. Parents should encourage their
children and raise them to follow God. Children sometimes forget that their parents are worthy of honor; they forget that learning from their parents' experiences can be very valuable. Parents
sometimes forget that children must often make their own mistakes and learn from their own experiences.

In "Father and Son," two messages are sung on top of each other
and never connect. What a powerful way to say that parents and
children don't listen to each other. A vital part of any relationship is the ability to hear and understand what the other person
is saying. Parents should make sure that they truly listen to their
children. Similarly, children should make sure that they take the
time to listen to their parents. Don't allow your family relationships to become a set of melodies that are sung over each other
and never connect.

Follow It Up

"Cat's in the Cradle," Harry Chapin
"In the Living Years," Mike and the Mechanics

 # Flowers Are Red

• • • • • • • • • • • • • • • • •

Harry Chapin (Chapin)
Living Room Suite
Elektra Entertainment
1978

Crank It Up

Harry Chapin describes what would happen if a young, growing mind in a young, growing body had an old, stagnant teacher. Imagine the lines you could not cross or the stories you would not read. Our world has little respect for imagination and many people wish to maintain the status quo. Our schools have turned into mulching piles rather than greenhouses. There is no way to calculate how much progress and creative thinking has been squelched because of a simple "It's not the time for art, young man; and anyway, flowers are green and red."

Talk It Up

- What's your favorite part of school? Why?
- Who was your least favorite teacher in elementary school? How about now?
- What qualities do you really appreciate in a teacher?
- When did you feel a light being turned on inside you because of a supportive teacher?
- What kind of teacher would you be?

Look It Up

The following passages are some examples of Jesus' teaching. Read each passage to discover what lesson was being taught. How did Jesus teach to ensure that his disciples learned it and not merely heard it?
Matthew 9:9–13
Matthew 13:1–23

Matthew 17:1–13
John 8:1–12
John 13:1–9

Wrap It Up

One of the greatest images of Christ is as a teacher. Never has the world seen a teacher as charismatic or creative. Never has a teacher made such an impact on his students.

Too often, teaching takes the form of information given, information heard; information memorized, information learned. There is a great assumption that hearing and memorizing are the same thing as learning. Christians today rely too heavily on that model when teaching the Word of God. Not only is it a poor form of teaching, it is also a real turnoff to someone who is unfamiliar with God's love.

Educators today would certainly agree that learning must be active and creative. It must take into account the student and his or her views. And it must last. Christ did all these things and more—he added the element of love. Jesus deeply loved those he taught. He wanted the Word of God "burned on their hearts." Then he wanted them to go out in the world and do likewise. We, too, are to go out in the world and teach others as creatively, actively, and lovingly as the Master Teacher taught us.

Follow It Up

"To Sir with Love," Lulu
"We Don't Need No Education," Pink Floyd

# Forever Young

• • • • • • • • • • • • • •

Rod Stewart (Stewart, Cregan, and Savigar)
Out of Order
Warner Bros. Records
1988—Reached number 12

Crank It Up

Bob Dylan wrote this song in the '70s and it's been redone a number of times over the years. Rod Stewart's version has more of a Top 40 sound, but the theme remains the same. Dylan's lyrics encourage us to look at life like a child and keep our innocence intact. "May the good Lord be with you down every road you run . . ." sings Stewart in the first line, and he continues to give instructions through the song on ways to remain "forever" young.

Talk It Up

- What is your earliest childhood memory?
- Would you like to return to a younger age? Which one? Why?
- What advantages are there in being young? What are some disadvantages?
- Do you want to stay young or grow up? Why?

Look It Up

1 Timothy 4:12. Do people think less of you because of your age? Why do they do that? Do you set examples in loving? faith? clean thoughts?

Mark 10:13–16. In what ways do we need to be more childlike? What do you think Jesus means when he says to come to him like little children?

65

Wrap It Up

The Spanish explorer Ponce de León searched diligently for the Fountain of Youth. The cosmetic industry spends billions searching for a formula to retain youthfulness. Advertising glorifies the youthful image. The message is loud and clear: Youth is beauty, beauty youth.

But aging is inevitable. Our bodies will slowly wear out. Our eyesight dims. Our hearing goes. Our mind and spirit, however, are not subject to that same process. People with aged bodies often possess great minds and light spirits. The mind is capable of retaining youth even when the body slides to ruin.

It is possible to preserve the joy and wonder that are usually only attributed to youth. We can be as happy at eighty as we are at twenty-five. We can dream and be visionaries at ninety-five as well as we can at sixteen. We can love and serve at any age. Cosmetics can't keep us young; but developing and keeping our soul in tune with our Creator can.

Follow It Up

"Forever Young," Diana Ross
"Forever Young," Bob Dylan
"Turning Thirty," Randy Stonehill*

From a Distance

Bette Midler (Gold)
Some People's Lives
Atlantic Records
1990—*Reached number 2*

Crank It Up

This song is about the difference between the way we look at each other and the way God looks at us. His perspective is much more accurate than ours. He sees things from a distance; he sees the big picture. But that does not mean he is distant from us; though each of us may be only a tiny part of the vast cosmos he has created, he not only sees us—he also recognizes the beauty and worth in each of us.

Talk It Up

- Who were your favorite baby-sitters when you were young? What made them so good (in your estimation)?
- Do you think God is watching over you? Do you feel like he knows you personally or not?
- Are there things in this world you wish God would look at a little more closely? Why?
- Are there areas of your own life you don't want God to see? Why?

Look It Up

Psalms 113, 116, and 121. What promises are given in these psalms? How do they reflect God's desire to protect, preserve, and strengthen us with his presence? Make two lists. On one, list your problems. On the other, write how you think God feels about each problem. Does he see? Does he care? Is he baffled by the problem or uncertain about the solution?

Wrap It Up

Julie Gold's lyrics remind us that everything can be viewed from two perspectives. The first is the up-close look. This view can give us fine details. We gain specific information from this perspective. What this perspective doesn't tell us, however, is how and where all the details fit.

The second perspective is the big picture. It enables us to see the whole or the finished product. However, the big picture fails to reveal details. Thus, one perspective without the other is often faulty. When we use only the up-close perspective, we may draw conclusions that are inaccurate or false. When we examine the big picture, we may miss details that give depth or meaning.

Only God can truly see the big picture. Only he knows the future and the purpose of events and people. It is our task as Christians to refrain from judgment until we have spoken with God, because his perspective is much wider than ours—big enough for the world and small enough for us as individuals.

Follow It Up

"No One Knows My Heart," Susan Ashton[*]

 # The Great Adventure

• • • • • • • • • •

Steven Curtis Chapman
    (Chapman and Moore)
The Great Adventure
Sparrow Records
1992

Crank It Up

Our lives need adventure to give us inspiration. We have let the routine and commonplace become all too familiar. With our long-faced religion determining our decisions from a list of dos and don'ts, we enjoy only a portion of the life God has planned for us. Steven Curtis Chapman sings about the great adventure that is ours in Jesus. By saddling up our horses and blazing new trails, we experience the pleasure of living in God's amazing grace.

Talk It Up

- What's the most daring thing you've ever done? Why did you do it? How did you feel afterward?
- What are some daring spiritual adventures you've taken? What are some trails you'd like to blaze?
- What scares you about doing things you've never done before? Would you enjoy having others come with you? How do you get others to come along with you?
- How has following Christ been an adventure for you? Is it important to go on these great adventures? Why or why not?

Look It Up

1 Corinthians 2:9–10. What things could these verses be talk-ing about? What might God have prepared for you? What are some of the deep things of God? How does God tell us where we should go?

Ephesians 2:4–10. What are some of the ways God shows his grace to you? What are some good works Jesus wants us to do? How do you tell the difference between those things he has planned for you and those he hasn't?

Wrap It Up

A man wrote a magazine article about a day he spent with his son. He was determined to do everything his two-year-old son did. If his son skipped down the drive, the man did too. If his son stooped to watch an ant, the man did too. After an hour, the man had to stop because he was exhausted. Yet during that hour, the man had seen and experienced God's creation in a way that he had long since forgotten.

Children are great adventurers. In their eyes, the most trivial things hold excitement and promise. They go deeper and farther into their experiences than any adult, drawing joy out of ordinary events. New Christians often possess that quality. They explore their new faith as if they were embarking on a great adventure. They joyfully anticipate each new discovery. Mature Christians often smile knowingly at such enthusiasm and comment that the excitement will wear off. They may even go so far as to say the spirit of adventure cannot possibly last over time. But why not?

Life in Christ is the most awe-inspiring, exciting life a person can experience. There is so much to learn and to discover. We are invited to share in the very life of Jesus, to participate in his ministry, share in his glory, and tap into his power. What an adventure!

Follow It Up

"Let's Go," Eric Cherry
"Hope Set High," Amy Grant*

 # The Great American Novel

Larry Norman (Norman)
Only Visiting This Planet
Phydeaux Records
1972

Crank It Up

This song is a discourse on the ironies of American life. Singing of the KKK, starving children, and Vietnam, Larry Norman points out the failings of a supposedly Christian nation. The chorus states, "The money says 'In God We Trust,' but it's against the law to pray in school." The song continues, but just as the listener begins to feel that America is quite hopeless, Larry Norman states the solution simply and completely: "I don't have the answers, I only have one. A man leaves his darkness when he follows the Son."

Talk It Up

- What do you consider the most serious problems facing America today? Which ones affect you personally?
- What solutions are the secular schools, government, and other institutions offering? How effective do you think such solutions will be?
- What solutions is the church offering? How effective do you think such solutions will be?
- Are there any problems you think are incapable of being changed? Why or why not?
- Do you expect any of those problems to be solved in your lifetime? Why or why not?

Look It Up

Ecclesiastes 12:8–14. Solomon, the author of these words, had been given wisdom by God. In this passage, Solomon announces the conclusion of his search for the meaning of life. What does he conclude? How does Solomon's conclusion compare to Larry Norman's prescription for America's problems?

Romans 12:1–2. What does this passage tell us to do? How can we renew our minds? How does that apply to Larry Norman's lyrics?

Wrap It Up

The world does not make sense. It is full of inconsistencies. People say one thing but do another. Laws that are written to protect sometimes hurt. The issues of the day are often highly complex. Sometimes Christians feel they need to solve all the problems and have all the answers; they join picket lines and boycotts. Unfortunately, we too often get caught up in mere activism.

Although solving society's problems is important, Christ called us to be fishers of men. The ways of the world are dark. The author of the song says, "A man leaves his darkness when he follows the Son." We are called to give that answer to the world. It is the only answer that will truly help.

Follow It Up

"Sign o' the Times," Prince
"Boy in the Bubble," Paul Simon
"American Pie," Don McLean

Hammer and a Nail

Indigo Girls (Saliers)
Nomads Indians Saints
Epic Records
1990

Crank It Up

A lot of groups talk about action but never do a thing. Without those people who actually move the dirt, raise the tools, and do the construction, we would just be talkers. Sometimes it is best to just get up and begin to *do* something, rather than going to more committee meetings or signing more petitions. This song celebrates those who take action and do something to change the world.

Talk It Up

- How good are you with tools? Have you ever built anything? What would you like to be able to build?
- How hard is it to get yourself going on a project? Are you more of a dreamer or doer?
- What things need to be built, repaired, painted, or cleaned in your neighborhood? How hard would it be?
- What things do you want to accomplish before you graduate? What kinds of action steps would it take to achieve these goals?
- What things are you involved in now to better your world? What things would you like to be involved in?

Look It Up

James 2:14–17. How would you apply these verses to yourself? Do you exhibit faith *and* works? Could you be doing more? What keeps you from doing your part?

2 Corinthians 8 and 9. These chapters depict "hammer-and-nails" Christianity. What actions are mentioned? List them. What ways could you be helping to make life better for others?

Wrap It Up

One of the most moving scenes in the movie *Witness* is the barn-raising scene. The whole order of Amish people come together to build a neighbor's barn. Each member has his or her role, from pounding nails to feeding the workers. In a single day, the barn is nearly completed. It is a startling testimony to what people can accomplish if they pick up a hammer and a nail.

Our society has drifted toward pessimism. We are quick to say we can't before we even try. It has been left up to visionary individuals and organizations to get us going. Habitat for Humanity proved that low-income housing could be constructed efficiently by volunteers working together.

Christianity is an active religion. It is more than belief or a philosophy. It requires action in order to grow. The Bible tells us that faith without works is dead. It doesn't say works produce faith; but true faith should produce good works. If your Christianity feels dull and boring, it is probably because you are ignoring its call to action. God can't make things happen if we don't pick up the hammer and nail.

Follow It Up

"If I Had a Hammer," Peter, Paul, and Mary
"It Isn't Love Till You Give It Away," Michael W. Smith

Have I Told You Lately

Rod Stewart (Morrison)
Vagabond Heart
Warner Bros. Records
1991—*Reached number 1*

Crank It Up

This beautiful Van Morrison lyric sung by Rod Stewart will more than likely become every young couple's theme song. With its tender affirmation, the words speak for our grateful hearts. "You fill my heart with gladness, take away all my sadness . . ." is just what we need to hear from our caring loved ones.

Talk It Up

- What does it feel like to be told you are loved?
- How often do you tell people you love them? Is it easy or hard to do?
- What people ease your troubles and fill you with gladness?
- Do you think you should become more verbal about your affection? Why or why not?
- Could this song be sung to God? Why or why not?

Look It Up

John 15:9–17. What words do you most often use to express love? What are your favorite ways for others to show you that they care about you?

Mark 2:1–12. Has anyone ever done something like this for you? What extent will you go to in order to help someone?

Luke 10:30–37. Who do you most rely on in times of need? When your friends are in trouble, what ways do you find it easiest for you to help? What do you do when you see a stranger in trouble?

Wrap It Up

This song is a love song, a thank you card, and a prayer rolled into one. Imagine how you would feel if this song was written to you. What a tremendous amount of encouragement you would feel. People who are encouraged and affirmed can scale to great heights.

When we feel that our work or efforts aren't appreciated, we often become angry. We may even feel bitter and unloved. Perhaps we should take our eyes off ourselves and examine the number of times we have thanked or encouraged someone else.

One of the saddest things that takes place in any relationship over time is the significant decrease in the number of times we state the obvious. In the beginning of love relationships, we can't say or hear "I love you" enough. We are constantly seeking new ways to express the sentiment. But once the commitment is made, we get back to the process of living. We assume the other person knows how we feel. "Of course she knows I love her; I married her, didn't I?" Or, "They know I appreciate them; they're my parents." The truth is, she isn't sure and they don't know.

We need to thank the people who have made a difference in our lives over and over and over again. We need to tell them specifically what it is that makes us appreciate them. We need to encourage them. It is not difficult to do; take David's lead. He wrote a whole book of praise songs simply telling God that he was aware of his presence, that he appreciated his involvement, and that he loved him. Have you told anyone lately that you love them?

Follow It Up

"I Honestly Love You," Olivia Newton John
"Shower the People," James Taylor*

Hello Big Man

Carly Simon (Simon and Wood)
Hello Big Man
Warner Bros. Records
1983

Crank It Up

It's hard to imagine our parents being anything but our parents. Yet they had to be young once. They once drove too fast and ate too much and stayed up too late. They once met and fell in love. This song is about Carly Simon's parents and how they met. It's nice to think that we are the product of our parents' love and devotion to each other; that we exist because two people felt an attraction for each other and acted on it. That day should be high on our list of wonderful moments in history.

Talk It Up

- How did your parents meet? Where? When? Did they fall in love at first sight? Where did they go on their first date? How long did they date? (If you don't know any of these things, try to find out this week.)
- What do you think your parents were like when they were your age?
- What kind of family background did your parents come from? What jobs did they have? Where did they live?
- What plans did they have for a family? What sacrifices did they make?
- How did your dad let your mom know he loved her? How did your mom let your dad know she loved him?

Look It Up

Philippians 2:1–4. How might these verses apply to husbands and wives?

Ephesians 5:21–33. According to these verses, what kinds of things are husbands to do for their wives? wives for their husbands?

Genesis 2:18. This passage shows that God decided man would be better off with a wife. Why do you think God felt that way?

Wrap It Up

One of the greatest gifts parents have to give their children is their past. A lifetime of living has given them numerous truths and lessons to pass on to their children. Their experiences in love, in friendship, and in learning can be invaluable. Unfortunately, this gift is also one of the greatest sources of tension in a family.

As children grow and mature, they begin to experience the world in new and varied ways. Each new experience brings a set of decisions to be made. Sometimes the child will make good decisions and the experience will be positive. Sometimes the child will make bad decisions and the experience may have negative outcomes. Throughout his maturation into adulthood, the child will continue to make choices and decisions.

It is the parents' job to guide the child toward experiences that will help him or her mature into a well-rounded adult. Unfortunately, parents are not given a book of instructions on how to do this. Most of parenting is based on trial and error and a strong desire to protect and shield the child from all that is bad in the world. Thus the parents use their past experiences to try to influence the child's decisions.

Tension arises when the child doesn't want the parents' input; this is not necessarily bad. A part of growing up is learning to be independent and responsible for your own decisions. On the other hand, God has given us a valuable source of information and expertise in the lives of our parents. To completely disregard it would be foolish. Take advantage of the wisdom that comes from experience.

Follow It Up

"Leader of the Band," Dan Fogelberg*
"In the Living Years," Mike and the Mechanics

 # Heroes

● ● ● ● ● ● ●

Commodores (Richie and Jones)
Heroes
Motown Record Co.
1980—*Reached number 54*

Crank It Up

We are fascinated by the famous (and even by the infamous). We also are intrigued by the unusual. But those people who get up every morning and do their jobs to protect us, govern us, teach us, and guide us are the true heroes of our day. We need to be more grateful to them and acknowledge how their efforts make our lives more satisfying.

Talk It Up

- When you were a child, what did you want to be when you got older? What do you want to be now? Why?
- How familiar are you with those people who do small things in your life? Do you know your mailman? gas station attendant? fireman? police officer?
- Why are we so fascinated with celebrities? Why are we so disappointed when they let us down? Should athletes be role models?
- How can we let our heroes know we appreciate them?
- What are some "heroic" things you do?

Look It Up

Look up these people and discuss what makes them heroes. What heroic qualities did each display?
Ruth 1:1–22 (Ruth)
1 Samuel 17:1–58 (David)
Esther 3:1–7:10 (Esther)
Daniel 3:1–29 (Daniel)
Acts 6:1–7:60 (Stephen)

Wrap It Up

"Say it ain't so, Joe" has become the catch phrase for fallen heroes. It refers to a comment directed at Shoeless Joe Jackson after he was banned from professional baseball for allegedly fixing the 1919 World Series. Countless celebrities and athletes have been berated for failing to live up to their hero status. A few have fought back by saying they never wanted to be a hero. Unfortunately, heroes have little say in the matter. Whether they wanted to be a hero or not, their status brings with it certain responsibilities.

The same is true for Christians. God gives us responsibilities that come along with the privilege of being his people. He calls us to be heroes. Heroes that stand for truth without wavering, present a strong and consistent example, and acknowledge the source of our strength and wisdom.

The Bible is full of heroes: Daniel stood strong in the lions' den; Esther's courage saved a nation of people; Paul endured hardship to spread the gospel. Today's heroes are not only the famous. Heroes are also the grandmothers who pray continually. Heroes are adults who refuse to cheat and lie to get ahead in the workplace. Heroes are teens who maintain their standards in the face of peer pressure. You encounter heroes daily. You may even be one.

Follow It Up

"We Don't Need Another Hero," Tina Turner
"Mrs. Robinson," Simon and Garfunkel

 # Hold On

• • • • • • • •

Wilson Phillips (Phillips)
Wilson Phillips
SBK Records
1990—*Reached number 1*

Crank It Up

This talented trio, daughters of superstar parents (Brian Wilson of the Beach Boys and John and Michelle Phillips of the Mamas and the Papas) emerged quickly on the music scene. With this song, we know why. Their tight harmonies and moving lyrics rival the old supergroup, Crosby, Stills, and Nash.

This song is about persevering amid struggles. If we can hold on for just one more day, we can handle the problem with strength. Endurance is a quality few have or even appreciate.

Talk It Up

- What do you think is the worst thing that could happen to you?
- What situations in life do you hope you never have to face?
- How does one more day make a difference?
- Are you good at holding on? Why or why not?
- What chains are holding you down now?

Look It Up

James 1:2–4. How do we benefit from pain? Why should we hold on?

Psalm 14. What does God do for those who call on him? What should our response be?

1 Corinthians 9:24–27. How might these words help us hold on? What reward for perseverance do these verses mention?

Wrap It Up

From the moment a baby is born, he or she possesses several innate reflexes. One of them is called the palmar grasp. If you stroke an infant's palm, he will automatically close his hand, grasp your fingers, and hold on tightly. From the moment of birth, God equips us with an instinct to hold on. That reflex, however, is developmental; it disappears after a few months. As we grow and mature, we need to regain that will to hold on.

A growing suicide rate and the advent of assisted suicide demonstrate that we are a society that has forgotten how to hold on. Advances in technology have conditioned us to believe we shouldn't have to face pain or struggle; perseverance is seldom rewarded. In fact, we applaud those who find the shortcuts.

Unfortunately, there are not always going to be shortcuts. Cancer treatments are still a lengthy process. Emotional wounds take time to heal. Physical rehabilitation may take years. Education is a lifelong pursuit. If we do not learn to persevere, we will be ill-equipped to face many of life's circumstances.

The Bible contains the greatest examples of perseverance. Scripture records how godly men and women held on to their beliefs, persevering in the most daunting circumstances. Those heroes were able to persevere because they knew they were not alone; God was holding on right along with them.

Hold on. Hold on for one more day. Remember that God is always with you. When the day of change does come, you will celebrate not only the end of your struggle but also the strengthening of your soul. Run to the end of your race. Stand tall in adversity. Finish your educational goals. Keep your promises to your friends. Hold on. Hold on for one more day.

Follow It Up

"You're Only Human (Second Wind)," Billy Joel*

Home by Another Way

James Taylor (Taylor and Mayer)
Never Die Young
Columbia Records
1988

Crank It Up

When we think of the magi's visit to the young child Jesus, we think of the miracle of the star and their adoration of the boy King. James Taylor uses the visit to teach us a different lesson. The Gospel of Matthew says that the wise men went home by a different way in order to avoid the evil King Herod. While Taylor takes liberties with the biblical story, he reminds us that we too need to steer clear of dangerous situations—and questionable company.

Talk It Up

- What major changes have happened in your life over the last five years?
- How does it make you feel to change plans after starting on a trip? How do you handle detours? What is your favorite route to school? least favorite?
- How do you handle evil people around you?
- Who are the King Herods in your life? What does it mean to "steer clear of royal welcomes" and "avoid a big to-do"?
- Do you steer clear of questionable company? How?

Look It Up

Matthew 2:1–12. What would you have done if you were the wise men? How did God warn them? How might God warn you of evil?

1 Peter 3:11. What should we do when we are around evil?

1 Peter 5:8. Why does Peter describe the devil as a lion in this verse?

Wrap It Up

It is always intriguing to hear the perspective of a mainstream musician who writes and records a song that centers strongly on Christian themes. We usually think of "Christian" songs as being sung by "Christian" musicians. Yet these songs are sometimes more insightful because the artists do not let themselves be limited by traditional interpretations of biblical events. James Taylor sees the story of the wise men as a call for us to be wary of the evil in the world. We should follow their example and change our course to avoid those who would trip us up. The experiences of the wise men give us some excellent examples of how to accomplish this.

The first thing we learn from the magi is to give the purpose of our journey first priority. The wise men kept searching until they found the child; they did not let themselves be swayed by Herod's flattery and lies. We too need to define the purpose of our journey and give it top priority. God wants us to live for him and base all that we do on that priority.

The second lesson of the wise men is to examine the motives of those around us. They were able to discern that Herod's motives were selfish and evil. Often, we find ourselves in dark and bad situations and we are baffled as to how we sank so low. We should simply take a good look at those around us. If we don't pick and choose our friends carefully, we could find ourselves in places we never wanted to be.

Finally, the wise men teach us the wisdom of changing our way. We tend to stubbornly cling to our old ways and old friends when we ought to "go home by another way." We need to avoid temptation and dangerous situations. It may mean avoiding certain friends or changing old habits. We may have to get home by another way. Let's "keep a weather eye to the chart on high" and arrive at our destination.

Follow It Up

"Better Wise Up," Amy Grant
"Leave Your Coat and Run," Eric Cherry[*]

# Hope Set High

Amy Grant (Grant)
Heart in Motion
A&M
1991

Crank It Up

This Amy Grant tune is about anticipating something good to take place. She sings, "If there's anything good that happens in life, it's from Jesus." She knows the importance of recognizing God's role in our lives and how he is responsible for filling us with his joy and wisdom. Putting our hopes in focus can make an incredible, life-changing difference.

Talk It Up

- What are your highest hopes and goals for your life? For the coming year? next month? this week? tomorrow? tonight?
- Is there any difference between a hope and a dream? If so, what?
- How excited do you get when you come to things like youth group meetings? Why? How would it change for you if you came more ready to learn?
- Why do you come to youth group meetings?
- What needs to happen tonight in order for you to feel like your time was well spent?

Look It Up

Joshua 10–13. Examine the battles of Joshua and determine if his expectations had much to do with his victories.
Mark 2:1–12. What examples of hopes set high are exhibited by these men?
Matthew 9:19–22. How did the woman's hope save her?
Matthew 8:5–13. What examples of hope are shown here?

Wrap It Up

There is an old corny tune called "High Hopes." The first stanza of the song says, "Just what thinks that little old ant; thinks he'll move that rubber tree plant. Everyone knows he can't, but he has high hopes." The song stresses the belief that even impossible tasks can be completed if you think positively. In the classic children's story, *The Little Engine That Could,* the engine pulled the train to the top of an impossibly high hill by chanting, "I think I can, I think I can."

The Bible is filled with examples of people who witnessed miracles because they had high hopes and strong faith. Joshua would have never marched around the city blowing his horn if he hadn't thought God would cause the walls to tumble. The Israelites would not have wandered in the desert for forty years if they hadn't had trust in God. The woman who touched the hem of Jesus' garment was driven by hope.

People today find it hard to set their hopes high. They believe those who point to the scientific advances of the day as evidence that miracles are impossible. They become unable to tap into God's most awesome power—his ability to do the impossible.

Christianity cannot be proven by scientific method; it is based on faith. We set our hopes high with belief that God will be faithful to his promises and even do things we had not even dreamed of. Keep your hopes set high. God will not disappoint you!

Follow It Up

"The Great Adventure," Steven Curtis Chapman*
"Let's Go," Eric Cherry

 # I Am a Rock

Simon and Garfunkel (Simon)
Sounds of Silence
Columbia Records
1966—*Reached number 3*

Crank It Up

This classic Simon and Garfunkel tune is about the need to be involved with people and with their lives. We try hard to protect ourselves from each other by building walls and isolating our movement to allow limited contact with others. Paul Simon uses irony to try to convince us that a rock feels no pain because it feels nothing; an island never cries but it never laughs, either.

Talk It Up

- What was the longest you've ever been alone? the longest you've ever been quiet? How did it feel?
- Do you think we look up to celebrities who symbolize individualism and independence (such as Clint Eastwood, Sylvester Stallone, and Arnold Schwarzenegger)? If so, why?
- What kinds of things are hard to enjoy by yourself? Why?
- Do you know anyone who has insulated himself from others? Do you ever do that? In what ways?
- When was the last time you cried in front of someone?
- How emotional of a person are you? Would you like to be more emotional?

Look It Up

Matthew 18:20. Why do you think Jesus said "where two or three are gathered?" What's the significance of this verse?
Romans 12:4–5. Does this verse relate to Paul Simon's song? If so, how?

Matthew 10:1. Why do you think Jesus chose twelve disciples? Why did he send them out in pairs? How might that apply to our discussion?

1 Corinthians 12:12–25. Why do you think Paul used the human body to illustrate how we need each other?

1 Thessalonians 5:11. How can you obey this verse?

Galatians 6:2. Why does Paul ask us to bear each other's burdens?

Wrap It Up

An old movie, called *The Man Without a Country*, told the story of a man who was found guilty of treason and was sentenced to live the rest of his days at sea. He could no longer call his (or any other) country home. He was truly an island. The movie chronicles his passage from defiant rebel to desperate recluse searching for a sense of belonging.

In many ways, we are like that man. We start out defiant. We are confident we can manage on our own. We view independence as a sign of success. We find, however, that our independence is often lonely. We discover that, as Nehru said, "It is a dangerous thing to isolate oneself; dangerous both for an individual and for a nation."

The Bible very clearly encourages us not to forsake the fellowship of others. The first gift God gave to Adam was a companion. Jesus sent the disciples out two by two. Paul traveled with a companion. God knows that we need each other for support and encouragement.

We need to work on our people skills. We need to be accessible to those who need us. We also need to learn to reach out to others with our needs. If we can be there for others, then they will be there for us . . . and those islands will have bridges and those rocks will be able to speak.

Follow It Up

"Lean On Me," Bill Withers*
"Lonely Boy," Andrew Gold
"At Seventeen," Janis Ian*

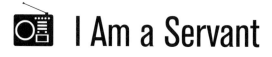 # I Am a Servant

Larry Norman (Norman)
In Another Land
Word
1976

Crank It Up

This classic Larry Norman song explores the nature of servanthood. The lyrics remind us that Christians are called to act as servants to each other. Our purpose in life is to please God by giving ourselves to each other. The song relates the testimony of a Christian who has failed. Renewing his commitment to God, he sings, "To live's a privilege, to love is such an art, and I need your help to start, oh please purify my heart. I am your servant."

Talk It Up

- Which would you rather do, serve or be served?
- Who is the most unselfish person you know?
- What does the songwriter mean when he says, "How can you choose me when you know I quickly fall?"
- How much of a servant are you? What do you need to work on?
- How does God feed your soul? How does he let you know he loves you?
- In what situations are you most likely to be a servant?

Look It Up

Galatians 5:13, 14. What ways can you serve others around you?

Luke 22:24–27. Are there any benefits to servanthood? What are they?

John 13:1–17. Have you ever had your feet washed? If so, what was it like? Is it hard to let someone wash your feet? Why?

Wrap It Up

Many Christians appear adept at acting like a servant. They give to missionaries. They donate money to charities. They may adopt a family at Christmas. But unless they also develop the attitude of servanthood, they aren't servants.

Far too often, people serve with conditions attached. "I will teach but I won't teach fourth grade." "I will give this money if they will spend it this way." "I would give, but these people don't appreciate it." Such "servants" place themselves on a level above everyone else; they pat themselves on the back as they reach down to those in need.

That's not what Jesus had in mind when he told us to serve one another. We are to humble ourselves by placing ourselves below those we serve. We must feel their need, their despair, and their longing. To be a servant is to walk among the hungry, the dirty, the lonely, the hurting, and the sick. It is to feel what they feel. It is to offer both physical and spiritual healing. It is a humbling and rewarding experience to wash the feet of another; so look around you for those who are in need and begin to serve in whatever fashion is best. Your soul will be fed as you feed the souls around you.

Follow It Up

"MLK," U2
"They Killed Him," Bob Dylan*

 # I Believe in You

Bob Dylan (Dylan)
Slow Train Coming
Columbia Records
1979

Crank It Up

Feelings of doubt and uncertainty always follow when a person becomes a Christian. Speaking from his own experience, Dylan crafts a message of determination and persistence. "I believe in you even through the tears," he sings, affirming the ability of faith to withstand the difficult times in life. Dylan covers the ground from which doubt may arise and encourages us to rely on the simple and plain expression of faith, "I believe in you."

Talk It Up

- What is your earliest memory of your Christian experience?
- Have you ever experienced doubt? What kinds of situations cause you to feel the most doubt?
- Who helps you keep your faith intact? What do they do?
- What can you do to fight the times of doubt when they come?
- How can doubt help you to become stronger in your faith?

Look It Up

1 Corinthians 13:12. How does knowing more help us to doubt less?

Matthew 14:22–33. What caused Peter to doubt? What causes you to doubt? How does having more faith cause us to doubt less?

John 20:29. Why is it difficult to believe in a God we cannot see?

Hebrews 12:2. What strategy does this passage give for over-coming doubt?

Wrap It Up

Our feelings of doubt are not something to be embarrassed about. All believers experience doubt at some time in their lives. We are especially susceptible to doubt during times of difficulty. Doubt is serious and can be damaging, but it is nothing to be afraid of. We don't have to bury our doubt, afraid that others will find out. Someone has said that doubt is the shadow cast by faith. Our assurance in Jesus comes no matter what degree of doubt we feel. We reply like the father in Mark 9:24, "I do believe; help me overcome my unbelief!" (NIV). Dylan simply leaned on his first response when difficulties arose, "I believe in you."

Follow It Up

"I'll Carry On," Rich Mullins
"This Is My Passion," Margaret Becker

Song to My Parents (I Only Want to See You There)

Keith Green (Green)
For Him Who Has Ears to Hear
Sparrow Records
1977

Crank It Up

In this personal cry made public, Keith Green sings to his parents. In a tone that is part apology, part explanation, and part evangelistic, he sings, "It's only that I care. I only want to see you there." With his passion for the unsaved meshing beautifully with his love for his parents, we are treated to the greatest desire a person can have for another. Keith Green puts into words what should be our hope for all of our unsaved family and friends.

Talk It Up

- Who in your life is not a Christian?
- What do you think the chances are of them becoming Christians?
- What would it take for them to make a commitment? How can you help?
- What are you doing to influence others for Christ?
- Would it make a difference if the person you were trying to influence was either of your parents?

Look It Up

Luke 14:15–24. What do you think is the point of this parable? Does it apply to you and your family? If so, how?

1 Timothy 4:12. What can you do to show your parents and siblings the love of God? Does it make a difference when you are younger than the person you are witnessing to? What strategy do you think will work best with parents? brothers? sisters? others?

Wrap It Up

Keith Green was a musician who sang God's messages. Every song he wrote was designed to proclaim God's truth. He made no exceptions or apologies. He did not back away from or temper his beliefs. He was passionate about saving the lost. Apparently that included his parents.

Nothing is more frustrating than to have someone close to you not share in something that is central to your existence; if you are a Christian, your relationship with Christ is central. It's natural to want to see your loved ones in heaven—and to share the joy of salvation on earth, too. But knowing that a loved one needs God and being able to tell them are two very different things.

Sometimes witnessing to family is harder because we are too close to them. Our flaws are readily seen. Keith Green admits in the song, "I'm such a bad example." However, we must realize that, while we must strive to be good witnesses, it is Christ we want our families to have faith in, not us.

Of course, often our families will answer no. That should not stop us from asking the question over and over again. The Master closed the doors to the wedding feast because the people received the invitation and still refused to come. According to the Bible, that will happen. God will close the doors and say, "I knew you not." Our hope is that those we love will accept the invitation long before the doors are closed.

Far too often, we become frustrated and angry with our loved ones. How can they not see? This is when we need to drop to our knees. Without prayer, none of our evangelizing, pleading, or begging will be effective. God can soften the toughest heart, open the closed eye, and quiet the tormented soul. We need to envelop our families in a cloud of prayer. We need to allow God to work in us and through us. Finally, we need to realize that God may choose not to use us at all. It doesn't matter who he uses to get through to our loved ones; all that matters is that in heaven we will greet that friend, that parent, that brother or sister, with outstretched arms and hugs of joy.

Follow It Up

"First Family," Rich Mullins
"Dear Friend," Charlie Peacock

I Still Haven't Found What I'm Looking For

●●●●●●●●●●●●●●●●●●●●●●●●●

U2 (Hewson, Mullen, Clayton, and Evans)
The Joshua Tree
Island Records
1987—*Reached number 1*

Crank It Up

The constant desire to find purpose in life will keep us moving forward, hoping to stumble across our own personal mission statements. We are never satisfied with who we are or even with what we've accomplished; part of us always yearns for more. This song is about the search to fulfill that yearning. U2 sings about what it feels like to always be searching for something you can't find. As they describe all that they have experienced without finding peace, a sense of hopelessness builds.

Talk It Up

- What things have you lost within the last month that you can't seem to find?
- What relationships from your past would you like to renew?
- When are you most dissatisfied with yourself?
- What kind of things are you searching for? How can you end this search?
- For what will you always be looking until you die?

Look It Up

Luke 15:11–24. For what was the prodigal son looking? Did he find it?
Ecclesiastes 12:13–14. The entire Book of Ecclesiastes details Solomon's search for meaning. These verses record what he found after searching wisdom, riches, pleasure, work, and

education to find purpose. Do you agree with his conclusion? Why or why not?

Matthew 7:7–8. What promise does Jesus give us if we seek?

Wrap It Up

When U2 came out with this album, Christians began to sit up
and take notice. Here was a secular band on the rock charts singing
about spiritual matters. The one thing that sets U2 apart from
contemporary Christian music is that most of their songs have a
"still searching" feel to them. This makes some Christians uncom-
fortable. Christians are supposed to have the answers. Searching
implies doubt. Doubt implies an imperfect Christian.

We mislead ourselves if we fail to recognize the prodigal son in
ourselves. All of us at one time or another have felt as though we
were missing something. Everyone has spent some time searching in his or her life. Solomon, with all his wisdom, spent his life
searching for truth. Finally he realized that life was meaningless
without God. You can't find anything if you don't look for it. Jesus
tells us to seek, then we shall find. Searching is not wrong; when
we fail to search we eliminate the chance of finding God.

Follow It Up

"Lord Is It Mine," Supertramp*
"Like a Rolling Stone," Bob Dylan

I Want to Know What Love Is

Foreigner (Jones)
Agent Provocateur
Atlantic Records
1985—*Reached number 1*

Crank It Up

Many of us are familiar with Foreigner songs without knowing it. They practically owned the pop charts in the late '70s and early '80s. Their songs blended catchy lyrics and thumping rhythms. However, this song differs from many of their other pop songs. It has an almost spiritual sound to it, with the choir singing in the background and Lou Graham fronting with his yearning voice. It would not be too surprising to hear this song being sung in the corner church on Sunday morning, expressing the age-old desire, "I want to know what love is."

Talk It Up

- What ways do you most enjoy being told you're loved? How do you show love?
- When was the loneliest time of your life? How did you get through it? Did anyone help you?
- How did you meet the group of friends you hang with now? Did you take the initiative or did they?
- Do you know anyone who needs to be shown what true Christian love is? How can you help them?

Look It Up

Look at Jesus' example to the people around him and how he showed them love. Discuss ways we can do the same in our circle of influence:
John 3:3–16
John 4:4–30
John 5:1–9

John 6:1–14
John 8:1–11

Wrap It Up

The current divorce rate in America is one out of every three marriages. That rate increases significantly in the entertainment industry. Among celebrities, it seems that divorce is the norm while stable marriages are considered an oddity. Whenever I read of another Hollywood marriage, I wonder if the couple plans on being together for life. Do they really love each other? Are they sincere in wanting to be together "till death do us part"? Are they surprised and devastated at divorce? The ironic thing is that the very people who show love so poorly are the ones showing and telling the world what love is.

Music, TV, and movies give us a strong indication of what the entertainment industry thinks love is. It is conditional: As long as you do this, I will love you. It is mystical: Love at first sight is extremely common. It is sexual: The "love" depicted in the media is based on sexual attraction.

Ancient Greek (the language of the New Testament) used four different words to express different kinds of love: *eros* (erotic love), *phileo* (brotherly love), *storge* (familial love), and *agape* (selfless love, the love of God for humanity). Unfortunately, today's entertainment industry portrays love only as *eros*. The sad fact is that *eros* is the least fulfilling and most fleeting type of love.

Agape, the love of our Lord, is the love that gives meaning to the emotion. It is an unconditional, deep, forgiving love; he loves us in spite of our faults and ugliness. It's a father's love in all situations. It's God's love, a sacrificial love demonstrated by the death of Christ on Calvary. No human love can duplicate it.

Human love can build on it, however. Love that is based upon a foundation of *agape* is capable of achieving the depth we so often seek. When we allow God to love us, we allow him to also love through us. Thus, our love for our brother *(phileo)*, our love for our family *(storge),* and our love for a member of the opposite sex *(eros)* become true love *(agape)*. Christians know what love is. We need to tell the world.

Follow It Up

"Show Me the Way," Dennis DeYoung[*]

If Your Heart Belongs to Jesus

● ● ● ● ● ● ● ● ● ● ● ● ● ● ● ● ●

Mark Lowry (Cloninger and Greer)
The Last Word
Word
1993

Crank It Up

Mark Lowry is a comedian/singer/entertainer. His routines poke fun at everyday life and usually add a little zinger to shake up our faith. In this song, he humorously reminds us that doctrine and denomination do not determine the depth or sincerity of our Christianity. He reminds us that regardless of what church you attend, all that really matters is that you have Jesus in your heart.

Talk It Up

- List as many denominations as you can.
- Can you describe any of the denominations in one word? two? three?
- Do you think we need denominations? Why or why not?
- What sort of things do you need to have in a church you attend?
- What things would not matter to you?

Look It Up

   1 Corinthians 1:10–17. How do you think this passage applies to the church today? How does it apply to you?
   1 Corinthians 3:1–23. What was happening in the church? What does Paul mean by saying he laid a foundation and someone else was building on it? How should we view other churches and denominations?

Wrap It Up

Only people could take a promise as simple as salvation and turn it into a complex mass of rules and regulations. Each Christian denomination is really a set of beliefs and traditions around which worship is created. For over two thousand years, humanity has come to love those rules and traditions so much that individuals would sacrifice their lives to preserve them. But it's not the rules we make that are so important. We must build our churches on the foundation Christ gave us.

The church of Jesus Christ is one church, not many. Every true follower of Christ is a member of that one worldwide church, regardless of whether he or she is a Baptist, Lutheran, Pentecostal, or something else. If everything is stripped away, we are still left with the fact that Jesus Christ is our Savior. Any church that is not built on that foundation should be avoided.

Christianity is a unique religion in that it is for all people of all races and cultures. God has given us a gift that transcends all of our differences. Denominations are extremely important in the spreading of the gospel of Jesus Christ. Once we all understand that, we can share our differences and rejoice in the fact that we all have Jesus in our hearts.

Follow It Up

"Mississippi Squirrel Revival," Ray Stevens
"Church," Lyle Lovett[*]

Imagine

John Lennon (Lennon)
Imagine
Capitol Records
1971—Reached number 3

Crank It Up

John Lennon's signature song was recorded at a particularly turbulent time in our nation's history. The Vietnam War divided the nation. We had lost promising political leaders to senseless assassinations. The Woodstock generation was still looking for answers in drugs and "free love." People were beginning to take a long look at themselves and the changes that years of protest and unrest had wrought. John Lennon's lyrics sound a plea for the world to try to live in peace with each other. He asks us to imagine a world with no heaven and hell, no wars, no religion, no hunger, and no greed—his personal vision of paradise.

Talk It Up

- What kind of world would you think of as a perfect world? What things would you eliminate? What things would you add?
- What do you think of Lennon's perfect world? Do you think he's right in saying that someday the world will live as one?
- How would you describe heaven? How does that differ from our common perception of heaven? How would you describe hell?
- Do you think heaven is possible on earth? Why or why not?

Look It Up

What insights do the following verses give to what heaven will be like?
Psalm 8
Psalm 19

Psalm 16:11
Daniel 12:3
Matthew 5:12
Luke 12:37
John 17:24
Acts 7:49
1 Corinthians 2:9
Hebrews 8:1
1 Peter 1:4
Revelation 7:16

Wrap It Up

All of humanity's existence has been spent laboring to improve the quality of life. We delve into complicated research to find ways to prolong life. We spend thousands on advanced technologies to improve our physical surroundings. We argue and theorize to find the best political circumstances. We explore religions and philosophies to find peace of mind. We seem to be constantly reaching for that one more thing that will bring us happiness.

John Lennon thought that if we banished all government, all religion, and even all ideas of heaven and hell, we would be happy. It would be wonderful to live in a world free from war, greed, and hunger. But a world without God and the promise of heaven would be far from paradise.

Communism sought to create utopia. It banned religion and set up a government in which the people would not have to take part. It sought to abolish class systems. Its professed aim was to create a society of happy, free people, but it failed miserably. Even a free society cannot achieve utopian perfection because it is composed of people—imperfect, faulty, sinful people.

Lennon was mistaken to think utopia could be achieved outside of heaven, because only heaven can make imperfect, faulty, sinful people whole and complete. Imagine that. I think you can do it if you try.

Follow It Up

"UFO," Larry Norman[*]
"Heaven," Bebe and Cece Winans

 # Innocence Lost

● ● ● ● ● ● ● ● ● ● ● ● ● ● ●

Susan Ashton (Kirkpatrick)
Angels of Mercy
Sparrow Records
1992

Crank It Up

The bottoms of our feet have diverse textures of skin. Tough, thick, hardened, almost leather-like skin grows around the heel and ball. Only a few centimeters away is the tender, baby-soft skin in the middle of the foot. Wayne Kirkpatrick's lyrics talk about how some of us have gone from soft, tender, sensitive, innocent people who live with passion to hardened, tough, calloused people who live with stubborn caution. Sometimes, wanting the innocence back is enough. We become fresh again with renewed vision. We need to regain our childlike spirit so we can experience life to the fullest.

Talk It Up

- What things do you lose most often?
- What is Susan saying she can't find? What do you think that means?
- What are signs that you have lost your innocence? regained your innocence?
- How stubborn are you? What issues are you most stubborn about?
- What does it mean to be teachable? Are you?

Look It Up

Mark 10:13–16. What did Jesus do in this passage? Why did he do it? What qualities do children have that we don't?
Romans 8:16. We are children of God; how can we reflect maturity and still keep our childlike innocence?

Matthew 18:1–6. What changes need to be made in your faith
to become like a child?

Wrap It Up

If you have ever spent time with a child, you know that the
world they see is very different from the world we see. Their world
is full of wonder, awe, and joy. They laugh more and with pure
delight. They experience their surroundings with every sense tin-
gling.

They believe in miracles and hope for the future. Their innocence is fully intact. In fact, it is their innocence that sets them
apart from us. As we get older, we look back at our childhood as
a magical time; we sigh and view it as a nice memory which did
not survive the march of time, but, is it memory? Can our innocence survive through adulthood?

Jesus rebuked the disciples for keeping the children from him.
He told them that it is the children who will inherit the kingdom.
He wasn't talking about children in terms of age; he was talking
about childlike souls. God wants us to maintain childlike qualities throughout our lives. He wants us to wonder and rejoice in
his creation. He wants us to believe the impossible and accept the
illogical. Ask him to take away your calloused, calculating heart
and replace it with one that beats like a child's.

Follow It Up

"The End of the Innocence," Don Henley*

 # It Is Well with My Soul

• • • • • • • • • • • • •

Wayne Watson (Spafford and Bliss)
How Time Flies
Word
1992

Crank It Up

This upbeat arrangement of an old church hymn strikes a chord in each of us. Whether we are singing to a church organ or Wayne Watson's drumbeat, the words speak of a peace that we all seek, a peace that is possible even amid strife and struggle.

Talk It Up

- Are you satisfied with yourself? Why or why not?
- What was the last thing you were totally satisfied with? Why that?
- What areas of your life bring you total satisfaction? Why those?
- What areas of your life do you struggle with most? Why? How do you handle it?
- Does your relationship with God affect how you handle problems? How?

Look It Up

Philippians 4:10–13. What is Paul's "secret of being content in every situation"?

1 Timothy 6:6. How do you react to this verse?

Hebrews 13:5–6. In what areas of life do we find it hard to be content? In what areas of life does God think we should be content? How does God expect us to handle chaos and confusion? stress? stillness?

Wrap It Up

"It Is Well with My Soul" describes a peace that is rooted so deep nothing can disturb it. It's a feeling nearly everyone seeks, but few ever find it. The key to the contentment talked about in the song is having a soul that is at peace. It is well with my soul. You can work to find peace of mind or physical relaxation—and may even feel at peace—but it is only temporary. It is only when deep down in your soul you have peace that you find lasting contentment. During times of struggle and heartache, your mind may be whirling and your physical body hurting. You will have to reach deep within yourself to find an anchor to give you some stability.

To make our souls right, we have to turn to the Creator of souls—God. Only God can change our souls. God makes no promises regarding our circumstances or our physical bodies, but he promises to take care of our souls. It is only when we give our souls to God for nurture that we can weather life's storms.

When all is said and done, all that really matters is our souls. Our souls will be left when all else passes away. When we truly believe that, we can put life's activities in their proper perspective and enjoy the life-sustaining peace God gives.

Follow It Up

"Let the Wind Blow," The Imperials
"All That You Have Is Your Soul," Tracy Chapman*

 # It's a Hard Life

Nanci Griffith (Griffith)
Storms
MCA Records
1989

Crank It Up

Nanci Griffith gives us a closer look at the ugly side of life in a world with little respect for itself. With bigotry, racism, and deception, we have offered little of the good life to our children. If we continue to give them bad examples to follow, "A hard life is all that they'll know." This song blames our present sad situation on the past wrongs of many adults who have promised a Disney World lifestyle to their impressionable children.

Talk It Up

- When is hatred most noticeable to you? From whom does it come?
- How do you feel about the KKK and other racist groups?
- What causes you to dislike people without even knowing them?
- Have you ever been judged without a chance to defend yourself? How did it feel?
- If you could change one thing about your life, what would it be?

Look It Up

John 4:1–10. This passage refers to an interracial animosity that persists even to this day. What is it? How did Jesus react to it?

Luke 9:51–56. Does racism reveal itself in this passage? How? How did Jesus react to it?

Luke 10:25–37. Why did Jesus choose a Samaritan as the hero of this story? What point did he make by doing so?

Wrap It Up

Racism and prejudice are not unique to today's world. They were alive and just as destructive in the time of Christ. What this song laments is that we just keep passing our prejudices from generation to generation, eliminating hope for the future. The sad part is that two thousand years ago, God's Son demonstrated how to live a life without racism or prejudice. Yet we continue to consciously or unconsciously perpetuate our prejudices.

In Genesis, we are told that God created us in his image. It does not say physical image, ethnic image, or socio-economic image. It must sadden God to see his children make those images more important than his own. He even gave us a model in Jesus Christ for loving others unconditionally. It is up to us to make sure future generations don't experience the "hard life."

Follow It Up

"One Tin Soldier," Coven*
"Signs of the Times," Sting
"Jackie Brown," John Cougar Mellencamp

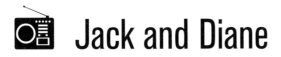 # Jack and Diane

• • • • • • • • • • • • • •

John Cougar Mellencamp (Mellencamp)
American Fool
Riva Records
1982—*Reached number 1*

Crank It Up

This song describes a typical midwestern couple who find them-selves trapped in a battle of freedom versus tradition. They are try-ing to get more out of life than merely surviving. Jack and Diane have grown up in every high school throughout the heartland and with a little nudging, you could probably figure out their last names. This typical guy and girl want something important to mark their lives as special. John Mellencamp paints a depressing "no way out" picture of this pair, "who are doing the best that they can."

Talk It Up

- What would you say to Jack and Diane if they were special guests at your high school?
- What would you say to Jack privately? Diane? their friends? their parents?
- Do you really think Jack and Diane are doing the best that they can? Why?
- What do you think Mellencamp means when he says, "The Bible Belt comes and saves our souls and makes us women and men"?
- What would you like to say to Mellencamp about being a teenager that he might have overlooked in his song?
- What predictions do you have for Jack and Diane for when they reach the age of thirty?

Look It Up

Ecclesiastes 12:1–5. What pattern should be set early in life? How will this affect a person's later years?

1 Timothy 4:12. What examples should we set? How can we do this?

2 Timothy 2:22. How would this passage fit into Jack and Diane's story? In what ways would it affect the way they live?

Wrap It Up

John Cougar Mellencamp's song touches on two points. The first is sex. Most often we hear this issue discussed from every possible angle except the emotional angle. We may have the best of intentions and still succumb to lust in the heat of the moment. We need to acknowledge all the emotions that are involved with our sexuality—the need to be special to someone, the need to belong, feelings of guilt, the intensity of lust. Then we need to ask God to help us deal with those feelings in an appropriate way.

The second area that "Jack and Diane" alludes to is a belief that all young people hold at one time or another. It is the belief that adults are trying to control them. Mellencamp's answer is to "let it rock, let it roll" while you can. The Bible has another answer; 1 Peter 5:5 says "be submissive to those who are older." Granted, adults do tend to be controlling and it sometimes appears that they have forgotten what it feels like to be young. But the truth is most adults remember exactly what it feels like. They have the benefit of having experienced the consequences of their youthful actions and they want to spare young people that pain.

Follow It Up

"Young Boy, Young Girl," Rick Cua
"The Party's Over," Kenny Marks

 # Judas's Kiss

Petra (Petra)
More Power to You
Sparrow Records
1982

Crank It Up

With typical Petra flair, this guitar and drum-driven song examines the pain of the betrayal Jesus must feel when we turn from him, from Judas's kiss to our petty spiritual aloofness, from the prodigal's searching to our selfish rebellion. We continue his pain when we go our own way, looking for other answers.

Talk It Up

- What's the worst physical pain you have ever experienced? the worst emotional pain?
- Have you felt betrayed? If so, how did you react?
- Do you think we ever cause Jesus pain? If so, how?
- Have you ever wandered away from God? Have you ever willingly disobeyed him? How do you think Jesus felt at such times?
- How does your sin affect your relationship with Jesus? How do you make things right?

Look It Up

Matthew 26:47–50. What motives do you think Judas might have had for betraying Jesus? Why do you think Jesus welcomed Judas, knowing his intent?

Matthew 27:4–5. What does this tell us about what was going on inside Judas?

John 18:25–27. Why do you think Peter denied Jesus?

John 21:15–22. Was Peter's denial different from Judas's betrayal? If so, how?

Wrap It Up

The name of Judas has become one of the most despised names in history. Why? Perhaps because he committed a terrible act that we believe ourselves incapable of. Would we send Jesus to his death in exchange for money? Never! Yet how many times do we betray Christ? More than we are willing to admit. And when we do, is it any less painful to Christ than Judas's betrayal?

Every time we turn from God's grace and choose sin instead, we betray Christ. Every time we shrink from identifying ourselves with him, we betray Christ. Every time we remain silent instead of proclaiming God's glory, we betray Christ. It hurts every time. It hurts Christ and it hurts us. It hurt Judas so much that it drove him to suicide. Let this song remind you of the presence of Judas's kiss in your own life and make you more determined to be faithful to our Lord.

Follow It Up

"They Killed Him," Bob Dylan*
"Vincent," Don McLean*

 # Just the Way It Is

• • • • • • • • • • • • • • • • • • • •

Bruce Hornsby and The Range (Hornsby)
The Way It Is
RCA Records
1986—*Reached number 1*

Crank It Up

This song is about the way we mistreat people just because of their color, their age, or even their family background. Backed by his band, The Range, Bruce sings out clearly against such prejudice. We don't have to stand for it no matter how entrenched it may seem. "That's just the way it is . . . don't you believe it." It doesn't have to be that way. We can change things. It can start with us.

Talk It Up

- What forms of prejudice are you familiar with?
- Have you ever been the victim of prejudice? Describe the circumstances. How did it make you feel?
- What do you think makes people prejudiced? Do you think such people can change?
- Are you trying to change the way things are? How?
- Will things ever be the way God intended?

Look It Up

1 Corinthians 12:12–27. List all the various types of people and functions in a church body. Do we emphasize some parts (people) of the church body above others?

James 2:1–9. What form of prejudice is shown in this passage? What action is asked for? Have you ever witnessed this kind of prejudice?

Acts 10:34–35. How do these verses apply to our discussion?

Wrap It Up

When a person loses a body part due to disease or injury, they experience a strange phenomena called phantom pain. They will feel sensations (such as pain) as if that limb or body part were still present. That says something very important about God's creation. He created the human body with such intricacy that missing parts are missed greatly. The body was designed to act as one unit with each muscle, each bone, each nerve, even each cell playing a specific part.

God's church is like that too. It is a single body functioning to spread the news of Jesus Christ. Within that body there are many parts. Some of the parts are the various churches across the world. We often are quick to point out our own church's superiority. We can easily find weaknesses in other denominations. But they are a part of the body, nonetheless.

God's gift of Jesus Christ was for all people of all races, cultures, and socioeconomic status. A middle-class, white church may never reach an inner-city Hispanic family. A conservative, traditional church may never attract the bubbly outgoing soul who craves excitement. But the urban mission or the charismatic church down the road may be just the thing those souls need.

Yes, prejudice does exist. It is all too obvious between races. It is more subtle but no less dangerous when it centers on worship, personality, or socioeconomic differences. That is the way it is. But that is not the way it has to be. We have been given a new way to look at our differences.

Let's take the freedom to accept each other and our differences as a way to unite ourselves, not separate. As Jesus saw beauty and dignity in Samaritans, tax collectors, and lepers, we should begin to look at people the same way. Ask God to give us his compassion for his people. Ask him to give us his eyes.

Follow It Up

"My Father's Eyes," Amy Grant
"Signs," Five Man Electrical Band*

Leader of the Band

Dan Fogelberg
The Innocent Age
Full Moon Records
1981—*Reached number 9*

Crank It Up

In this song, Dan Fogelberg opens his family album for us as he describes his relationship to his father, and how he differed from his brothers. We follow Dan in his attempt to thank his father for his influence, for helping him find his purpose in life, especially in music. Dan's father loved music also, but had to give it up to keep his family together. His brothers chose different paths, but Dan chose to pursue music. He realizes that his passion for song was instilled in him by his father; he sings, "his blood runs through my instrument and his song is in my soul."

Talk It Up

- What career do you want to follow? What influence have your parents had in your choice?
- Have you resisted your parents' influence? Why or why not?
- Would you want your parents to be more directing? Why or why not?
- When was the last time you thanked your parents for their help? the last time you told them you loved them? How do you express appreciation?
- Has anyone besides your parents given you a passion for a specific career? Who? How did he or she do so?
- What kind of person do you need in your life right now to inspire you? What would your life be like if God were that person?

115

Look It Up

> *1 Timothy 4:12*. Has your father given you an example to help you live the right way? If not, has someone else?
>
> *Isaiah 58:11*. Do you ever feel God guiding you? satisfying you? strengthening you?
>
> *1 Corinthians 11*. Who are you following right now? Who is following you?

Wrap It Up

"Honor your father and mother" is one of the Ten Commandments that we often have trouble following. It would have been a lot easier if God had added some conditions stating "if" or "when." But he didn't. He said to honor them, period. Of course, some parents make it difficult for their children to honor them. Yet God says we must do so nonetheless, for it was through them that God created us. Fogelberg highlights another reason for honoring our parents—their gifts to us. Our talents, skills, and personality are given to us by God through our parents.

Fogelberg not only recognizes the need to honor his father, he shows us how. Can you imagine how his dad must feel when he hears Dan sing this song? Our parents make a lot of sacrifices and perform a lot of loving acts on our behalf. Yet they are rarely recognized or thanked. We are quick to blame our parents for their shortcomings; we should be equally quick to show our appreciation. We don't have to compose songs. A hug, a letter, or spoken recognition to friends will make any parent feel honored. Of course, some of us have the added blessing of other mentors—teachers, friends, ministers—who inspire and guide us. They deserve honor, too.

Follow It Up

"Have I Told You Lately," Rod Stewart*
"To Sir with Love," Lulu
"Second Fiddle," Eric Cherry
"In the Living Years" Mike and the Mechanics

 # Lean on Me

• • • • • • • • • • • •

Bill Withers (Withers)
Still Bill
Columbia Records
1972—*Reached number 1*

Crank It Up

This classic song about friendship and togetherness has been remade many times. With his "you-can-count-on-me" message, Bill Withers has crafted a song that challenges us to help each other in a time of need, but also to let others do the same for us.

Talk It Up

- Who has helped you out in your life the most besides your parents? What have they done for you?
- What are some ways that you enjoy being helped? What are ways you don't like to be helped?
- Are you better at helping or being helped? Why?
- What is going on in your life right now that you could use help with? What could someone do to help you?

Look It Up

Matthew 28:20; Philippians 2:1–11; 4:10–20. What assurances does God give us in these verses?

Philemon 1–23. How was Paul helped by the presence of Onesimus? In what ways was Onesimus helped by Paul? Did their relationship benefit anyone else? Who?

Wrap It Up

A friend can give no better gift than his or her presence and help in times of trouble. Just the knowledge of that presence is sometimes enough to pull us through. No one is able to live life alone. Throughout the Bible, God assures us that he is always with us, but God seems removed and distant to many people who seek a tangible presence. As Christians, we need to be there for people. We need to let them lean on us. Through us, they can feel the tangible love of God.

The flip side to this is that we are not just to be pillars for leaning. We are also to be leaners. We are not immune to the pain life throws us now and then. God has provided a fellowship of believers to help alleviate that pain.

Follow It Up

"You've Got a Friend," James Taylor
"Shower the People," James Taylor*
"Thank You for Being a Friend," Andrew Gold

Leave Your Coat and Run

• •

Eric Cherry (Cherry)
Just A Container
Stone Productions
1992

Crank It Up

In this quick-paced tune about Joseph and how he dealt with temptation, Eric Cherry gives us the best advice for those moments of sinful desire . . . leave your coat and run! This song about the lure of temptation details Joseph's encounter with Potiphar's wife in Genesis 39. "Leave Your Coat and Run" points out that we are made victims and not victors when we give in to temptation.

Talk It Up

- What are your most persistent temptations?
- When was the last time you gave in to temptation? What was the situation? Why then? How did it make you feel?
- What do you lose by giving in?
- How do you resist temptation best? How can you avoid defeat in the future?

Look It Up

Genesis 39:1–23. List the temptations Joseph faced. Make another list of the ways Joseph dealt with temptation.

Matthew 6:13. How should we approach temptation? What can God do for us when we are tempted? How does he do it?

1 Corinthians 10:13. What promise does God give us? Have you ever experienced God's help in confronting temptation?

James 1:12. What do we get for defeating the temptation? Does that motivate you to succeed?

1 Peter 5:8. How often are you tempted? Why so often? In what ways should your treatment of the devil be similar to how you would act toward a lion?

Wrap It Up

Comedian Flip Wilson created a character named Geraldine. Whenever she gave in to temptation, she would shrug and say, "The devil made me do it." When we fall prey to temptation, we are likely to give the same excuse. However, the devil does not make us do anything. He may tempt us, but it is our choice whether to give in or resist. When we do give in to temptation, it is usually because we make one of three mistakes: presence, procrastination, or premise.

A mistake of *presence* occurs when we allow ourselves to be in the presence of temptation for too long. It is easy to refrain from eating jelly doughnuts if there are no jelly doughnuts in the house; it is not so easy if jelly doughnuts sit out on the kitchen counter all day. The same is true of sexual temptation. It is easy to say no when you and your date are with a group of people; it's not so easy when the two of you are alone in a dark place. Eric Cherry's song reminds us to flee such situations. We must learn to identify and avoid circumstances where we are likely to be tempted.

Sometimes we give in to the temptation because of *procrastination*. We postpone our good intentions and continue to engage in sinful activity. "I'll start my diet tomorrow." "This is the last time I will ever drink." Unfortunately, tomorrow never comes and "last times" multiply. We must pledge to resist temptation and to start right now . . . not later.

We also give in to temptation at times because of a wrong *premise*. This premise is usually a rationalization so we feel better about our sinful acts. We tell ourselves that sex before marriage is okay because we love each other. We disregard the speed limit because "everyone else does." We drink, but it's okay because we never get drunk. Usually, we have to state the premises louder and louder because we know in our hearts that we're disobeying God.

To avoid temptation, we must recognize our weakness and pledge ourselves to do right without delay. We must flee temptation. There are no medals awarded for doing battle with temptation; but there is a crown for those who win. Joseph was right. Leave your coat and get out of there!

Follow It Up

"Go West Young Man," Michael W. Smith
"Dear John Letter to the Devil," Keith Green

Let's Wait Awhile

Janet Jackson (Harris III, Jackson, and Andrews)
Control
A&M Records
1986—*Reached number 2*

Crank It Up

This song is rare in modern music . . . a plea to wait for sex. Janet Jackson surprises us by expressing a conviction that later is better. Janet convinces her boyfriend that their love will remain if it is real and lasting. And with the wait will come the assurance of "stronger love not dependent on just physical attraction." This is a wise and well-written song from a somewhat surprising source.

Talk It Up

- Do you find it hard to wait for things?
- In a relationship, who do you think usually pressures the other into getting physical—the guy or the girl?
- Have you ever been pressured to go too far? How did you feel?
- What are the benefits of waiting? Why don't more couples see those benefits?
- What can a couple do to keep from going too far?
- What can a person do if he or she has already given in to sexual temptation?

Look It Up

1 Peter 2:11–12. How does lust affect our souls?
Galatians 5:24. What does it mean to crucify the flesh? Why does God want us to do that?
Titus 2:11–12. How do we deny lust? How do we keep it from gaining a hold in our lives?
1 Corinthians 6:18. What strategies can we follow to avoid sexual immorality?

Wrap It Up

Perhaps the most surprising thing about this song is who wrote and sang it. It is rare to find a celebrity in the entertainment world speaking out against premarital sex. Music, television, and movies so often consider premarital sex a foregone conclusion. Yet there are those who decide to wait awhile. *People* magazine once printed an article on the marriage of talk show host John Tesh and actress Connie Selleca (both are committed Christians). *People* was amazed that John and Connie chose not to have sex until they were married. What a sad comment on our society that we are more shocked by the obedience of a command than by the sin.

Such a choice seems odd to many, who ask, "Why wait?" John Tesh's answer to *People* was because God told us to. John and Connie waited because it was the right thing to do. There are many reasons to save sex for marriage: Such a commitment will bring about lasting pleasure, deliver from guilt and insecurity, and open the door to real intimacy. The bottom line, however, is that God told us not to have sex before marriage. Premarital sex is a sin. Waiting is not only the smart thing to do; it is also the right thing to do.

Follow It Up

"The Party's Over," Kenny Marks
"Young Boy, Young Girl," Rick Cua
"Jack and Diane," John Cougar Mellencamp*
"I Don't Want Your Sex," DC Talk

 # Lord Is It Mine

• • • • • • • • • • • • • • •

Supertramp (Hodgson and Davies)
Breakfast in America
A&M Records
1979

Crank It Up

This beautiful song is a prayer for those who are spiritually out of sorts. Each of us needs to find a place to retreat from the battle zones of life. Supertramp sings about doing just that. We all need a silent place that we can call our own.

Talk It Up

- What do you think the title of the song means?
- Do you have a place you enjoy going to just to sit and think and pray? Is it easier to pray there?
- What circumstances drive you to your retreat?
- Do you ever feel sad? wounded? tired? What happens when you feel that way?
- What things do you pray about most often?
- What does the song mean when it talks about "feeling your sweetness through the day"? How often does this happen to you?

Look It Up

Matthew 14:23; Mark 6:46; Luke 6:12. Why do you think Jesus went away to pray? What places do you have available to you for praying? Are there certain rules that you follow when praying?

Matthew 6:5–13; Mark 11:25; Luke 9:28; Luke 22:41. What instructions does Jesus give us for praying in these verses?

Wrap It Up

There was a song in the '70s sung by Three Dog Night entitled "One," that lamented the state of being alone. Our society has taken this idea to heart. We've come to view being alone as something truly awful. We fill our lives with people, activities, and noise to keep the silence away.

We will never be good at spending time alone until we understand why we need to have it. Jesus went off alone to spend time with God because he felt he had to. He did it because he needed it. He needed the strength only God could give. He understood that the fullness of God couldn't be reached in the presence of distraction. It was in the silence that he could hear God most clearly.

The same is true for us. We need the peace that only God can give us. But when we try to reach him in the midst of our busyness, we can't possibly hear him. We have forgotten how to listen. We need to discipline ourselves to find a time and place to be quiet. We need to practice speaking to God and listening for his response. Once we've heard God speak, we will find ourselves yearning for these times of aloneness.

Follow It Up

"Cool Change," Little River Band*

Love of the Common People

Paul Young (Hurley and Wilkins)
No Parlez
Columbia Records
1984—*Reached number 45*

Crank It Up

The encouragement that comes from a good mom and dad cannot be measured. We owe our parents a great deal for providing us with the basic essentials of life and letting us experience the pleasure of living while they do their best to keep us from its pain. A healthy, well-adjusted child will lead to a healthy, well-adjusted adult. Paul Young sings of how having a good family can soothe the wounds that childhood and adolescence often bring.

Talk It Up

- How would you describe your family? large? small? expressive? protective? supportive?
- Do you think your parents have sacrificed for you? If so, how?
- What are your family vacations like? Do they bring your family closer together?
- Does your family have any special traditions or customs? What are they?

Look It Up

Ephesians 6:1–4; Colossians 3:18–21. According to these verses, what are the roles of each member of the family? In what specific ways are these roles fulfilled?

Philippians 2. What ways does your family sacrifice for you? How do you sacrifice for them?

Wrap It Up

The family has come under tremendous attack in our society today. With a definition that is constantly changing, the exact nature of the family is difficult to discern. When former Vice President Dan Quayle commented on the impropriety of glorifying TV character Murphy Brown's pregnancy outside of marriage, a national furor arose. People became sharply divided over what constitutes a family. What the debate missed was that the definition of a family is not as important as the purpose of a family.

Families are all different, but what makes a good family is the fulfillment of the roles that God defined in his Word. Unfortunately, not all of us have families in which all members are willing to fulfill these roles. Yet as Christians, we still must strive to fulfill our part. Then with God's help, our families can change. The love of the common people that Paul Young was talking about is the love of God.

Follow It Up

"First Family," Rich Mullins
"Leader of the Band," Dan Fogelberg*

 # Luka

• • • • •

Suzanne Vega (Vega)
Solitude Standing
A&M Records
1987—*Reached number 3*

Crank It Up

Of the many unreported crimes that go undetected, child abuse ranks among the ugliest. This song is about a little child who is being abused on a regular basis. "Luka" stunned radio listeners when it first aired. The melody is haunting and the words are disturbing, prompting us to face a topic we might otherwise choose to avoid. Be very sensitive to the members of your group when you play this song.

Talk It Up

- What is the point of this song?
- Have you ever heard of anyone being physically abused? How did it make you feel? What did you do about it? What ended up happening?
- Are there ways of being abused without being hit?
- Have you ever been abused? What happened? Have you ever felt like you could have been very close to being abused?
- How might people respond to abuse?

Look It Up

Ephesians 4:31. How does this relate to abuse? How do we get rid of such things?

Proverbs 16:32. Do you know anyone who controls his or her anger well? Describe them.

Proverbs 22:24, 25. What are the dangers of being friends with hot-tempered people?

Ephesians 6:4. How are parents responsible for their actions?

127

Wrap It Up

When Gregory K., an eleven-year-old foster child, decided to divorce his parents so that he could be adopted by his loving foster parents, a furor arose from many pro-family groups. Those groups argued that the court was meddling in a sacred institution: the family. They were right; the family is a sacred unit. But many of them overlooked the sad fact that not every family is serving its God-given purpose. Gregory K.'s parents had repeatedly abandoned him, forcing him to live in a series of foster homes. Gregory never received the love and support of a family, an experience that is all too common for children today.

Children are among God's greatest gifts. They should be treated with respect and love. There are a lot of families, be they two-parent, single-parent, divorced, or even grandparents, who are living up to God's expectations. However, there are a lot of families who are not. The angels must weep as children are abused and neglected. To treat a precious gift in such a way seems unforgivable.

Yet, just as God forgives us, abusive friends and parents can be forgiven, too. However, forgiveness does not erase the consequences of their sin. God holds us responsible for our sin. But God is capable of turning bad to good; he can create wonderful families from single mothers, widowed fathers, caring grandparents, unrelated foster families, and even formerly abusive parents.

To be a parent is a privilege bestowed by God. When that privilege is abused, we must protect the gift.

Follow It Up

"Dear Mr. Jesus," Sharon Batts and Power Source
"Another Day in Paradise," Phil Collins

The Maker of Noses

• • • • • • • • • •

Rich Mullins (Mullins and Beaker)
The World as Best as I Remember It, Vol. 2
Reunion Records
1992

Crank It Up

This little-known Rich Mullins tune is about the quest for a perfect world. As we search along with Mullins, we find that the world's direction leads nowhere. The song lets us know that following our hearts, our noses, or even our dreams will send us down a dead-end road. Mullins concludes that it only makes sense to follow the Father of hearts, the Maker of noses, and the Giver of dreams.

Talk It Up

- What kind of traveler are you? Do you get lost easily? Do you use a map? Do you ask for directions or prefer to find your own way?
- Have you ever gotten bad directions? What happened?
- How can you discern good advice from bad? How do you determine when it is God guiding you? What keeps us from following God more closely?

Look It Up

Look at each character and determine when they were following God and when they were following their noses:

Jonah 1–4 (Jonah)
Job 3–10 (Job)
James 1:5–8. What role does God play in setting our goals?

Wrap It Up

The world is full of advice. Newspapers are loaded with advice columns. There are columns to answer your questions regarding your health, personal life, your garden, and even your pets. The nonfiction shelves of our libraries are full of how-to books designed to help us reach our potential. We can purchase crystals to tap into our inner energy. We can make an appointment with a medium who will put us in contact with a spiritual guide. We can learn to develop our leadership skills. We can find advice on just about any topic.

Such advice comes . . . and goes. Trends die out. Books fall off the best-seller lists. And we go on searching.

Only one "advice book" has remained a best-seller for centuries. The advice has remained pertinent over the years. Its wisdom rings true regardless of era, culture, or race. That book is the Bible.

If you truly want to achieve your potential, go to the source of that potential. God is your Creator; he alone knows what you can achieve. He knows your dreams. He alone can lead you to success. So slow down before him and ask for his guidance in your life. He is the only one who knows the perfect direction for you to travel. Drop your homemade maps to the ground and pick up his heavenly compass; he won't disappoint you.

Follow It Up

"The Great Adventure," Steven Curtis Chapman[*]

 # Man in the Mirror

Michael Jackson (Garrett and Ballard)
Bad
Epic Records
1988—*Reached number 1*

Crank It Up

This beautifully structured song from Michael Jackson gives a musical tour of some of the worst parts of our society. Our problems—homelessness, wars, and natural disasters—tempt us to abandon hope of ever changing our world into a place of peace and pride. However, Michael asks us to first take a look at ourselves—fixing up our world starts with each of us. We cannot hope to change the world unless we start with the man—or the woman—in the mirror.

Talk It Up

- How many times do you look in a mirror each day? What do you usually do most often after viewing yourself?
- What do you think Michael means when he says, "I'm starting with the man in the mirror; I'm asking him to change his ways"? What things need changing in your life?
- Do you find it easier to focus on your own shortcomings or those of others? Why do we want others to change more than we want ourselves to?
- What could you do as a gesture of good faith to help others change without being critical?
- Why don't we improve quicker than we do? How would your world improve if you overcame your greatest faults or problems?

Look It Up

2 Corinthians 5:17. What do you think it means to be a new creation? What "old things" pass away? What new things come?

Matthew 7:1–5. Is it hard for you not to judge other people?
   Why or why not?

Matthew 7:24–29. What would it take to change your life and
   put it on solid rock?

Wrap It Up

You can change your skin tone by visiting a tanning salon. You
can change the color of your eyes by purchasing tinted contact
lenses. You can change the shape of your body by visiting a diet
center or a gym. You can even make major body changes by visiting a plastic surgeon. A completely new you is possible!

You would think a world that is so adept at changing a person's
physical body would be at least somewhat advanced at changing
the inner self. Not so. Few people even talk about changing the
person inside. Yet larger muscles, a good tan, and a new nose will
not prevent violence or increase understanding among people. If
we want to make the world a better place, Michael Jackson says,
take a look at yourself and change your ways. Change the kind of
person you are. Change the way you act. Change the way you
relate to other people.

That's easier said than done, of course. But it's possible. Take
Paul as an example. He started out as a Christian-hating Jew who
persecuted and helped stone Christians to death. He experienced
a drastic change in his soul by a direct confrontation with Christ
on the road to Damascus. The new Paul spent the rest of his life
serving God and spreading the gospel around the world.

That type of change is not unique to biblical times. It can and
does happen today. People's lives have been radically changed by
the presence of God. Even those whose changes are not so dramatic have gone on to change the world around them. So take a
look in the mirror and start changing the world with the person
you see there.

Follow It Up

"Cool Change," Little River Band*
"Change in My Life," John Pagano*

Mountain of Things

Tracy Chapman (Chapman)
Tracy Chapman
Elektra Entertainment
1988

Crank It Up

The '80s was considered the "me" decade, a time when everyone tried hard to get as much of everything as they could. There comes a time, however, when "enough is enough" and we start to realize that "less is more."

Tracy Chapman came from meager surroundings and hit stardom rather quickly. In this song, she explains how our response to excess has crippled us into thinking the bigger our pile, the more we have to be pleased with.

Talk It Up

- If you won a million dollars in the lottery, how would you spend it? In what ways would your life change?
- Which of your possessions are off limits to anyone else? Why?
- How has money affected your life in good ways? bad ways?
- Why do so many people seem to lose touch with what's important after becoming wealthy?
- What level of income would satisfy you?

Look It Up

James 5:1–6. What warnings does this passage give to the rich?

1 Timothy 6:6–10. What can happen when we seek riches? How should we view the material things in our lives?

Wrap It Up

On all levels, our society desires *things*. Even Pepsi used the slogan, "Gotta have it." Yet when we get whatever "it" is, it is not enough: Soon we yearn to possess something else. We expend tremendous amounts of energy acquiring things in hopes of finding meaning or happiness. We have little time left over for developing our inner souls and connecting with other people. It's ironic that we spend so much time seeking material goods because they are only temporary. Our souls, on the other hand, are forever. Material objects are inanimate, incapable of giving love. We are animate human beings seeking acceptance and love. God showed us his love in the form of a man. That man was without material wealth. He is where we should direct our energy. His love will take us to the top.

Follow It Up

"Material Girl," Madonna
"Money Changes Everything," Cyndi Lauper
"Simple House," Margaret Becker

 # Mr. Wendal

• • • • • • • • • • •

Arrested Development (Speech)
3 Years 5 Months 2 Days in the Life of Arrested Development
Chrysalis Records
1992—*Reached number 6*

Crank It Up

This is a song about a homeless man named Mr. Wendal. He doesn't have a family and he eats out of the trash. But he does have his dignity intact. This song is part rap, part storytelling, part preaching. In their unusual style, Arrested Development sings about the need for progress in our attitudes and actions toward our unfortunate brothers and sisters.

Talk It Up

- Have you ever been homeless? Have you ever been hungry for a long time? If so, what was it like?
- Have you ever given money to a street person? Why or why not? Would you take money from someone if you were homeless?
- Do you think Mr. Wendal is a burden on society? Why or why not?
- Why do you think there are homeless people among us?
- Should we be responsible for the homeless? How should we respond to them?

Look It Up

Proverbs 25:21. If we should do this for an enemy, what should we do for the poor?
Matthew 25:40–45. How do these verses apply to us today?
Matthew 6:1–4. How should we help those in need? What are some ways to do that?

Luke 6:38. What happens when we give? Should that be our motivation? What happens when we don't give? Should that be our motivation? Why or why not?

Wrap It Up

One of the most sobering aspects of our generation is the significant increase in the homeless and the poor. Suddenly, suburbia is confronted with handheld signs begging for work right outside the local grocery store. Friends and relatives find themselves out of work as bills continue to mount. And these things occur in the middle of one of the most prosperous countries in the world.

What is the response of the Christian community? One would like to say that they have risen to the occasion, that they practice what they preach, that they have provided food, shelter, and comfort. The truth is, the Christian community seems to have done no more than the secular community in eliminating this problem. We all seem to have been struck dumb by the arising needs in our neighborhoods.

Mother Teresa was once asked in a documentary how she could be helped. She replied, "Just look around." There are many ways to help. We often waste time waiting for someone to tell us what to do. We must simply start helping. We need to give of our time, our money, our material goods, and ourselves.

Mother Teresa also illustrates another lesson. She does not serve the poor because she was moved by the sight of their plight on the streets of Calcutta. She was in a train on her way to a retreat when God spoke to her and laid out his mission for her. She serves because God told her to. God has also directed us to serve others. We should not wait to be moved by emotion. Being a Christian means being a person of action. Jesus helped the needy, not because he was supposed to, but because he loved them. We should do likewise.

Follow It Up

"Man in the Mirror," Michael Jackson*

 # Nick of Time

● ● ● ● ● ● ● ● ● ● ● ● ●

Bonnie Raitt (Raitt)
Nick of Time
Capitol Records
1989—*Reached number 92*

Crank It Up

Sometimes we get so anxious for things to happen in our life, we begin to think those much-looked-forward-to events will never happen. We anticipate graduation, college, marriage, and having children with such excitement that we sometimes fear they will pass us by. Bonnie sings about people who spend their lives waiting—and never do any living. She was afraid this might happen to her in the area of love. But after many years of restlessness, she says, she found love—"in the nick of time."

Talk It Up

- What's the "closest call" you've ever experienced? a near-miss accident? an almost-too-late term paper? something else?
- Are you afraid that some of life's good things might pass you by? If so, which things?
- How do you react when people talk about "God's timing"? Do you believe God has a specific plan for your life? Why?
- What are some things you feel God has in store for you? Are there any ways you can help God bring these things about?

Look It Up

Ecclesiastes 3:1–8. How do these verses apply to Bonnie Raitt's song? Is there a time to regret? When?

Matthew 25:14–30. Are you ever afraid of getting involved in something new? If so, why? Would you face risks? enjoy benefits?

Matthew 19:16–22. What do you think caused the ruler not to
follow Jesus? How are you like him? Does anything cause
you to hold back in your relationship with Jesus? If so, what?

Wrap It Up

"Anticipation. It's making me wait. It's keeping me waiting."
Carly Simon's song has become a theme across America. A ketchup
company even used it to tell us that waiting for the ketchup to
come out of the bottle is worth it. Advertisers often capitalize on
the powerful effects of anticipation. Promotions for the new fall
television programs start in July. News shows break into regular
programming to give us a news tidbit to hook us in for the regular broadcast. Everything is designed to build our anticipation.
The goal is to maximize our desire for the end product.

Anticipation is often a positive thing, but when all our energy
is directed to what may (or may not) happen in the future, we
jeopardize our present. That may be what happened to the rich
young ruler. He backed away from following Jesus because he
couldn't risk his future by obeying Jesus in the present.

In our own lives, we need to put our futures in proper perspective. It is great to have goals and dreams, but we must be careful to live in—and enjoy—the present.

Follow It Up

"Turning Thirty," Randy Stonehill*
"Veronica," Elvis Costello

 # No One Knows My Heart

Susan Ashton (Ashton, Sprague, and Kirkpatrick)
Wakened By the Wind
Sparrow Records
1991

Crank It Up

This beautiful song is about the intimate relationship we can have with God. Susan sings of the emotions and thoughts that can be masked from others. We pretend not to hurt. We pretend not to care. In the creation of our facades, we even pretend we enjoy the deception we act out. We can hide from everyone else, but we can't hide from God. He knows our heart better than anyone else, even ourselves.

Talk It Up

- What was your favorite Halloween costume as a kid? Why?
- How often do you pretend to be someone you're not?
- Who knows you best (besides God)? Are there things that even this person does not know about you? Why?
- Who would you like to have know you better? Why them?

Look It Up

Psalm 139. Go through this Psalm verse by verse and list the ways God is involved in our lives. Allow time for personal testimonies about God's presence in the lives of his people.

Wrap It Up

Count the people who *really* know you. Chances are, you can name no more than one.

By the time we reach adulthood, we have acquired numerous roles to play in our lives. We are the child to a parent, the friend of a peer, the love interest of another, the student or teacher, the employee or employer. The parent may not know the desires of the love interest. The peer may never see the disappointment of the child. The teacher may not know the fears of the employee.

Even we sometimes get confused by the roles we play. We may struggle to keep the roles separate, but we often lose sight of who we really are. One of the biggest risks we will take in our life is to share ourselves in a love relationship. In such relationships, we hope to reveal our true selves and still be loved. Unfortunately, sometimes we are afraid to reveal too much. Other times we are rejected by the other person. In both instances, the real person gets buried deeper.

There is one person, however, to whom we can reveal our heart. Right from the start, he lets us know that we will be accepted no matter what lies in our past. He tells us to expect love and encouragement to change our future. There is no role playing with him, because he sees past the roles. That person is God. He is willing to take all our pain, our fears, and the secrets of our heart. In return, he will fill the empty places with love. All he asks is that we turn to him and return his love. We want to be known and he wants to know us. The one who knows us best loves us most.

Follow It Up

"Innocence," Margaret Becker
"Make My Life a Prayer to You," Keith Green

 # One Tin Soldier

Coven (Coven)
Billy Jack
Warner Bros. Records
1971—*Reached number 26*

Crank It Up

This song, the theme from the hit movie, *Billy Jack,* tells a story about a group of people who possess a hidden treasure. They are attacked by another group of people who want this treasure. After much violence and tragedy, the attackers discover that the treasure was not what they expected. The treasure was simply the motto, "peace on earth." This story highlights the devious methods we employ to gather objects for our own good.

Talk It Up

- Is there anything you can remember always wanting as a child but never getting? Is there anything now you want but don't see how you could get it?
- What things do your friends own that you find yourself wanting? What would you do to get it?
- What does the song mean when it says, "Do it in the name of heaven"?
- Were you surprised to find out that the treasure in the song was peace on earth?
- What does "one tin soldier rides away" mean?

Look It Up

Exodus 20:17; Proverbs 21:26. What does it mean to covet?
1 Timothy 6:10. What happens when we covet? Who do we harm?
2 Samuel 12:1–14. What was the point of Nathan's parable? What things resulted from David's covetousness? Do you think David thought it was worth it?

Wrap It Up

Our society places tremendous emphasis on the things we have—or don't have. Clothing labels are status symbols. The cars we drive tell the world our place on the social ladder. We buy "starter" homes, a term that implies we will eventually buy something bigger and better. Our wants are never satisfied.

So what is the answer? To say "stop coveting" is too simplistic. We need to look at our lives and begin to assess what items we need to survive and what items are luxuries. We need to differentiate between want and need. When we feel that desire for something beginning to build, we need to step back and ask ourselves a few questions. Why do I want it? How will it meet my needs? Who will benefit from it? And, most importantly, how does God view it? That last question will require time spent in prayer. True discernment comes from God. If we fail to let him guide us, we will find ourselves in David's predicament. The cost of satisfying our desires without regard to the consequences is too great for anyone.

Follow It Up

"War," Edwin Starr
"Eve of Destruction," Barry McGuire
"I Do Not Want What I Haven't Got," Sinead O'Connor
"All That You Have Is Your Soul," Tracy Chapman*
"Desire," U2

 # Paper in Fire

• • • • • • • • • • • • •

John Cougar Mellencamp (Mellencamp)
The Lonesome Jubilee
Mercury Records
1987—Reached number 9

Crank It Up

Mellencamp has given us songs over the years that ring of truth in a dark, desperate way. This song is no exception; it points out the futility of having dreams and doing nothing to see them accomplished. From love to living the good life, we always seem to come up short of catching the brass ring. The vivid image of paper bursting into flames is a very accurate picture of what happens to us and our dreams when we fail to make our desires come alive.

Talk It Up

- What are common dreams of people your age?
- What are your dreams?
- Name some ways you can go about fulfilling them.
- What could prevent your dreams from being fulfilled?
- Do you have any dreams that have gone up in smoke like paper in fire? Can you prevent that from happening again? How?

Look It Up

Proverbs 3:4–6. What are some ways to trust God with your desires? How can you put God first?

Proverbs 2:1–9. What promises does God give us in this passage? How do they apply to your dreams?

Nehemiah 2:1–5. What was Nehemiah's dream? Did he accomplish it (Neh. 6:15)? How long did it take? What sacrifices did it require? How does Nehemiah's experience apply to you?

Wrap It Up

If you have a green thumb, you probably have a house and garden full of plants. If you don't, you may shrug your shoulders and laugh about your gift for killing plants. Of course, everyone knows that no one actually has a green thumb. If you have a houseful of plants, it's because you take time to carefully tend them. Plants die because they do not receive the things they need for life. Now with the advent of silk plants, we can all have a house full of plants with absolutely no care required. After all, no one should be denied the beauty of plants just because they can't or won't care for them.

We tend to view our dreams as plants. People whose dreams come true are lucky, just like someone who has a green thumb. For those of us who aren't lucky, we view our dreams as silk plants. It is our right to have them and we shouldn't have to nurture them.

John Mellencamp points out that when we view our dreams like this, we will see them disappear the way paper disappears in fire. Dreams, like plants, need to be planted, watered, and nurtured. We need the help of the Giver of life to bring them to life.

God earnestly desires to see us achieve our dreams. He makes the dreams possible much like he enables plants to grow. It is up to us to nurture our dreams and encourage their growth. It takes work to fulfill the potential God placed within us. Yet it will be worth the effort as one day we gaze around our garden of well-tended dreams. The harvest is worth the work. Don't be satisfied with silk plants when you can enjoy the beauty of real flowers in bloom.

Follow It Up

"Hammer and a Nail," Indigo Girls*

 # Patience

• • • • • • • • • •

Guns N' Roses
G N' R Lies
Geffen Records
1988—*Reached number 4*

Crank It Up

This Guns N' Roses tune is about taking it slower and using patience to mend and restore a relationship. Of course, Axel and the boys have lived their lives in the fast lane more often than not. It is all the more surprising, therefore, to hear this anthem about patience from a charter member of the pack.

Talk It Up

- Do you consider yourself a busy person? What things take up the most time in your life?
- Are you a patient person? What makes you impatient?
- Do you ever try to slow down and exercise more patience? How do you do that?
- When have others been patient with you? In what ways has God been patient with you?

Look It Up

James 1:2–4. How does pain develop patience in us? Have you experienced this?

Romans 5:3–4. What benefits do we get from patience?

Galatians 5:22. Have you seen the fruit of the Spirit in your life? If patience is a fruit of the Spirit, what does that suggest about how to develop it?

2 Peter 1:6. How is patience (or perseverance) a bridge to other qualities?

Hebrews 12:1. What can we do to run the race with perseverance (patience)?

Psalm 40:10. Have you ever sat silently and let God speak to you? What happened? How would your life change if you did this more often?

Wrap It Up

We live in a microwave society. Countless technological advances have made the pace of life faster. Speed dialing, cellular phones, remote controls, drive-thru windows, fax machines, microcomputers, cash machines, and fast food all strive to help us make better use of our time so that we will have more time for . . . for what? Why, to move on to the next thing, of course. We are so used to being busy that we do not know what to do when we have to wait. A driver would rather risk an accident and push through a yellow light than sit for three minutes until the light changes again. Three minutes!

So what have we gained? Not much, really. What have we lost? Perhaps our lives. Patience is not just a nice quality to have; it is vital to our spiritual growth. Look at the example Jesus gave us. He didn't teach as he and the disciples ran down the road. He usually sat them down, often away from the bustle of the towns, and then he taught them. When did he pray? He didn't only do it while he was preparing food. He usually went off by himself to spend time with his Father.

Most Christians lament over their lack of quiet time. We often hear advice designed to fit our busy world: Pray in your car on the way to work or pray while you dry your hair. Is it good advice? We may sometimes hear God over the noise of the traffic or hairdryer, but better advice would be to learn to be patient and quiet. We need to stop the frantic pace of our lives and wait on God.

Follow It Up

"Looking Through Patient Eyes," P. M. Dawn
"Busy Man," Steven Curtis Chapman*

📻 People Get Ready

● ● ● ● ● ● ● ● ● ● ● ● ● ● ● ● ● ●

Rod Stewart (Mayfield)
Storyteller: The Complete Anthology, 1964–1990
Warner Bros. Records
1989—Reached number 48

Crank It Up

This beautiful version of the Mayfield classic includes the fine guitar work of Jeff Beck accompanying Rod Stewart as he pleads with us to get ready for the train that's coming to take us to heaven.

Talk It Up

- Where is your favorite place to travel? What is your favorite mode of travel?
- According to the song, what should we get ready for? Why do you think the song says you "don't need no ticket"? How do you "get on board"?
- What do you think the song means when it says "there's no room for sinners"?
- Are you ready for Jesus to return? Why or why not? What should we do to get others ready too?
- Do you want him to return soon? Why or why not? Can we do anything to speed his return?

Look It Up

John 14:1–4. How does Jesus describe heaven? Do you think he makes it sound appealing? If so, how?

Acts 1:11. How does this verse describe Jesus' return? What do you think that means?

1 Thessalonians 4:13–16. What do you think is the point of these verses? How should we respond to the message?

147

Mark 13:24–29. What do these verses have in common with the song, "People Get Ready"? How can we get ready for Jesus' return?

Revelation 22:20. According to this verse, when is the "train to glory" arriving? What should we do in the meantime?

Wrap It Up

There is a strong fascination for Christians and non-Christians alike when it comes to the study of the end times and the Book of Revelation. Numerous predictions have been made concerning the nature and date of Christ's return. The whole subject often brings intense curiosity, combined with fear and trepidation. These are not the emotions one would think would accompany Christ's triumphant return. Perhaps it is because we have relegated this event to the distant future. We are able to speculate and explore the endless possibilities because it doesn't seem real to our present.

But the truth is that it could happen at any time. Jesus said he would come unexpectedly, like a thief in the night. We must be ready now. Being ready does not mean we must know the seven signs or identify the Antichrist; it means we must be ready to meet Jesus face to face. We must have our personal house in order.

How do we do that? We must recognize Jesus as the Son of God and believe that he died on the cross for our sins. We must believe that he rose on the third day and is in heaven preparing his coming kingdom. We must confess our sins and our need of him, and ask for his forgiveness and presence in our lives. Yes, it is simple, but it is also vital. There are no reasons to wait. There is nothing that needs to be done in order to accept his plan of salvation. Nothing will change with time, except the increased possibility that he will return when you are not ready.

Follow It Up

"UFO," Larry Norman*
"I Wish We'd All Been Ready," Larry Norman

People in a Box

Farrell and Farrell (Farrell)
Jump to Conclusions
Starsong
1985

Crank It Up

The average American household has two televisions. Many families plan their waking hours around their favorite shows. We have given over control of our creative thinking to people in a box. Farrell and Farrell's song accurately portrays many American families. We wake up with Joan Lunden and go to sleep with David Letterman. This song pins our TV habits to the wall and we are asked to look closely at what we have become . . . a spectator nation.

Talk It Up

- How many TVs are there in your home?
- How many hours a day do you watch TV?
- What shows do you watch every week? Why?
- Could you live without TV for a day? a week?
- Are you bothered by what is on your TV set in your home?
- How would your life change if your family got rid of all the TVs in your home?

Look It Up

Romans 7:22, 23. What keeps us from controlling our TV habits? What other habits are out of control?

Colossians 1:9. How can we fill our minds with good things? What are those good things?

2 Peter 3:1. What does a pure mind look at? How does that apply to our TV viewing habits?

Titus 1:15. Does this apply to our TV habits? If so, how? What shows would you place in each of the two categories mentioned in the verse?

Philippians 4:8. What shows fit this framework? What shows don't? What needs to be changed in your TV viewing?

Wrap It Up

Television has made an immeasurable impact on our society. It brought the world into our homes. It broadened our horizons. It enabled people to see things they had never seen before (and some things they might have never seen at all). At first this was a wonderful event. People treated it with the respect it deserved. People were aware of what TV had done for them and kept it in its proper perspective.

Through the years, TV has become so commonplace, nearly every home has one. Most have at least two. The cable industry has increased our choices of channels. With such a range of viewing choices, we can see many good things—and much that is not so good.

God must despair when he sees the influence TV has over us. He must grieve that we would put our highly creative and intelligent minds on autopilot and let a box do our thinking for us. TV is not the danger; it is what we do with it. We allow it to control our minds and senses, and so neglect the greatest gift God gives us—our ability to think.

We are responsible for taking care of our earthly bodies; we are likewise responsible to see that we develop all our senses. We need to fill our hearts and minds with holy things. We need to choose carefully the things that we see and hear.

Try this. Commit yourself to a visual fast. Fast from TV for a length of time. Use that time to give your eyes a visual feast of God's things, to challenge your mind with stimulating books or challenging projects. When you finish, check your ability to control your TV habits. If they are still out of control, then fast again. And continue to fast until you can master the machine. There are much more productive ways to grow than with a remote control. Let God give you strength to say no. He wants to set you free and make it possible for you to soar with eagles instead of being a couch potato.

Follow It Up

"57 Channels," Bruce Springsteen
"Money for Nothing," Dire Straits

 # Pine Box

• • • • • • • • •

Rossington Collins Band (Harwood)
This is the Way
MCA Special Products Records
1981

Crank It Up

This unusual song about death and how we look at it is performed a cappella, without noisy instruments surrounding the vocals. The starkness of the song communicates powerfully that we really don't need much after we're gone. "Don't give me no cold pine box, don't dig me a hole," he sings, leaving simple directions for those he leaves behind.

Talk It Up

- Are you afraid of dying? Why or why not?
- What kind of funeral do you want? music? speakers?
- What does the song mean? What does "prime your pump" mean?
- Why does the song use just voices and no instruments?
- What things are you wishing to hear "to strengthen your soul"?

Look It Up

1 Corinthians 15:55. What does death give us? Why can we look forward to death? Why are we more real and alive after we die?
Romans 6:7. What promises are made to those who trust Jesus?
Revelation 14:13. How do our deeds follow us?
John 11:25. What is required of us?

Wrap It Up

If you've ever been to a funeral home, you've probably heard some discussion regarding how the deceased looks. "They did a nice job," some will say. "He looks peaceful," others will comment. Despite such comments, people don't look the same in death. The hair color doesn't change; neither does the shape of the face or the color of the eyes. They look the same—and yet drastically different.

The difference is difficult to describe. There is no spark, no animation, and no clue as to who the person is or was. It goes beyond the absence of breath or of a heartbeat. What is missing is the soul. The soul gives definition to a person. The soul defines who we are, what we feel, and what we believe. God created our souls. He then gave them to us to care for and nurture in relationship with him.

We all have some fear of death. We fear physical pain. We fear the end of all that is familiar and the beginning of something unknown. Some people fear death because they are uncertain what will become of them. For these people, there is no assurance, no comfort, and no calm for the fear. After preparing our souls for death, we have something to help keep the fear at bay. We have the assurance of joy in the presence of our Creator. We can put our physical death in perspective and leave the pine box for those left standing at the graveside.

Follow It Up

"Dust in the Wind," Kansas*

Pressure

• • • • • • • • •

Billy Joel (Joel)
Nylon Curtain
Columbia Records
1982—Reached number 20

Crank It Up

We live in a pressure-cooker society characterized by fast food, rapid transit, and express mail. Even the youngest among us get caught up in trying to do everything and make everyone happy with us. After a while, we become consumed with keeping up the commitments we've made to others, going from one activity to another, fighting the clock, the traffic, the deadline. This song is about the pressure that comes from living in today's fast-paced, microwave society.

Talk It Up

- Do you ever feel pressure? When? What kinds of things cause you to feel pressured?
- How do you deal with stressful activities? Which is the best way?
- What benefits do you get from stress? Do you invite stress or avoid it?
- Do your parents handle stress differently than you? In what ways?
- What kinds of stress do you go through now that your parents didn't encounter until they were adults?

Look It Up

1 Peter 5:7. What does the Bible say about handling pressures?
Matthew 6:25–34. What does God do for us?
Matthew 11:28–30. What is a yoke? How do we put on God's yoke?

James 1:2–4. How does pressure affect us? Can we benefit from it? How?

Romans 12:2. How does the world pressure us to fit into its mold?

Wrap It Up

"Stressed out." It has become one of the most common phrases of our decade. Stress has become a way of life for many people, old and young alike.

Microwaves make cooking easier and quicker. Cordless phones increase our mobility. Computers now perform numerous tasks previously done by hand. Washing machines, dishwashers, trash compactors, and even supermarkets are all designed to save time and labor. Yet in spite of all these time-saving devices, we are more stressed than ever before. That's because stress doesn't come from outside influences, it comes from the inside. Stress is a direct result of the demands and expectations we place on ourselves as we try to conform to society's standards. We cause ourselves stress by choosing to try to live up to the standards and demands of others.

No amount of technology can enable us to meet those standards. They set up an ideal without taking into consideration every person's unique traits and talents. We place pressure on ourselves when we try to conform.

On the other hand, God is able to recognize each person's gifts and traits. He is able to see the person as a whole. His standards are based on his love for us and his desire to see us happy. When he allows us to experience pressure, it is for our good. God causes us to mature through the process. In effect, we are made whole in his shaping hands. Only God himself knows what we are able to withstand and how to use the pressures for our benefit.

Follow It Up

"Carry On Wayward Son," Kansas
"Busy Man," Steven Curtis Chapman*

Rachel Delevoryas

Randy Stonehill (Stonehill)
Stories
Myrrh Records
1992

Crank It Up

We all have childhood memories of picking on other kids for no better reason than how they looked. We said things, did things, and thought things that were cruel and unfair. Looking back now, we realize how mean and destructive we were and hope that time has been kind—kinder than we were—to those we have mistreated. This song reminds us of the pain we inflicted on the innocent so many years ago. We all know a Rachel Delevoryas.

Talk It Up

- Who was the one kid everyone picked on when you were little? Why did he or she stand out as different? How did he or she respond?
- Have you ever been picked on by someone for no good reason? How did you feel? How did you deal with it?
- Why are kids so mean to each other?
- Would you like to know how the kids you picked on turned out and whether they remember the pain? Why or why not?

Look It Up

Matthew 7:1–5. What do these verses mean? In what ways do we judge people? According to the passage, what is the danger in this?

Matthew 5:22. What does Jesus say the penalty is for calling someone a fool? Is it a fair penalty? Why or why not?

Luke 19:1–10. What kind of person was Zacchaeus? Do you think he was well-liked in Jericho? How did Jesus treat him?

155

Acts 7:59–8:3; 9:1–8, 23–27. What kind of person was Saul?
How did the church treat him after his conversion? How did
Barnabas treat him? What can we learn from the stories of
Zacchaeus and Paul?

Wrap It Up

We've all been there, part of a group teasing some unfortunate
soul. A battle rages within us: Should we defend the person or
remain a part of the group? More often than not, we keep silent.

The Bible says to judge not, yet we do it all the time. We are
continually classifying people. There are people we admire, people
who we model ourselves after, people who are not "our type,"
people who are not worth our time. And people we scorn. We do
it time and time again.

Yet Jesus did the exact opposite. He exasperated his followers
by the people with whom he chose to associate. He offended reli-
gious leaders by selecting common fishermen and tax collectors
as disciples. He defended confessed sinners. He defied all the rules
of society.

He did so because he had the ability to see every human's potential. He could see through the unlovable traits to what made that
person a much-loved child of God. It was his vision that enabled
the person to evolve and change.

We must seek to imitate Christ in that respect, and treat every
person as God's most miraculous creation. We must see them (and
help them see themselves) as God sees them. As we do this for
people, others will be doing this for us. Wisecracking, teasing, and
judging must turn into encouraging, inspiring, and loving. Then
those who have been thrown aside will feel the great joy of belonging.

Follow It Up

"Howard Grey," Ed Kilbourne

 # River of Dreams

• • • • • • • • • • • • • • • •

Billy Joel (Joel)
River of Dreams
Columbia Records
1993

Crank It Up

This title song from Billy Joel's most recent album was hailed by critics as a breakthrough for Joel. They felt it was an indication he had left behind his sugary pop style for more substantive songs. "River of Dreams" deals with Joel's search for meaning to his life. It is full of biblical allusions such as references to the valley of fear and the mountains of faith. The river of dreams symbolizes that chasm that stands between him and the promised land. Despite his attempt at spiritual depth, Joel backs away from the promised land in the end.

Talk It Up

- Does your life have a purpose? What is it?
- For what kinds of things do people spend their lives searching?
- What are the "mountains of faith" that give us confidence?
- What types of things dwell in the "valley of fear"?
- What kinds of things cause us to experience the "jungle of doubt"?
- Why do you think Billy Joel says only blind eyes can see what he is looking for?

Look It Up

2 Kings 5:1–10. Do you think "River of Dreams" evokes this passage? What is the significance of the river to Naaman?

Revelation 22:1–5, 14. What surrounds the river of life? How do you get to the heavenly city?

Acts 22:16. What significance does water have in Christian belief and practice?

Hebrews 10:22, 23. The picture in these verses is not of a river; what illustration does Paul use? How does it apply to us?

Wrap It Up

Christian hymns and spirituals feature countless allusions to the "river of life" that enables us to leave our sin and evil behind and enjoy paradise. According to Revelation, we will encounter that river when we enter heaven. According to that same passage, if we are washed in that river, we will gain access to the tree of life, to immortality, to eternity in paradise.

We all encounter a symbolic river at some point in our lives. We see the good on the one side and the bad on the other. Christ calls us to let the river wash away the bad and come to the good. It seems easy enough, but several things hold us back.

The first is the valley of fear that Billy Joel sings about. This fear may be tangible. It may be the fear to try something different or the fear of persecution. It may be the fear of losing ourselves, no matter how imperfect we are. Fear is a great paralyzer. It can hold us back from ever testing the waters.

The second obstacle is the jungle of doubt. We live in a world where all things must be proved. Issues of trust and faith are regarded with skepticism. Yet our spiritual lives must be built on faith. Belief is easy when the proof is readily visible. But belief based on faith requires much more courage. Billy Joel knows that it is this courageous belief he must have to cross the rivers. He says "it can only be seen by the eyes of the blind."

In the end, regardless of your fears and doubts, you will have to make a decision about the river. Don't be like Joel, whose indecisiveness allows the river to carry him into the ocean. Come to Jesus and use the river to wash away your dirt; then step clear to the other side. It is not a river of dreams. It is a river of reality, but we won't have to cross alone. We will have help. Jesus is calling us to not be satisfied with our simple questions and answers. He wants us to dream bigger and deeper, just like the river we must face in order to come through victoriously.

Follow It Up

"The Eagle Song," The Imperials
"The Logical Song," Supertramp

The Rose

• • • • • • • • •

Bette Midler (Mc Broom)
The Rose
Atlantic Records
1979—Reached number 3

Crank It Up

This haunting ballad is Bette Midler's definition of love. She recognizes that others sometimes view love as painful and dangerous. She also recognizes that we all have times when love seems so distant we think we can barely continue living. Midler, however, provides us with a different definition of love.

Talk It Up

- Who loves you? How do they show their love? Who do you love? How do you show your love?
- What different kinds of love do you have (love for parents, love for friends, love for boyfriend or girlfriend)? How are they different?
- Is love ever hurtful or painful? If so, how?
- When is love at its best?

Look It Up

Use the following verses to discuss the signs and effects of love. What insight does each give into the character of love?
1 Corinthians 13:1
Galatians 5:6, 13
Ephesians 3:17
Ephesians 4:16
Colossians 3:14

Wrap It Up

Psychologists, theologians, and even scientists agree that people must experience love in order to live healthy lives. A few years

159

ago, as news cameras viewed the Romanian orphanages, our nation was given a glimpse of what happens when there is no love. We were horrified. Small bodies had practically ceased to be children. Several news programs did before-and-after programs on the lives of these children. They would place pictures of a child while still in the orphanage alongside a picture of the same child after months of living with a loving adoptive family. The difference was dramatic. It was often difficult to see that they were actually the same children.

Everyone needs to be loved, but many are afraid of it. They may accept love from a parent, but they avoid love that must be worked for. Of course, there is a lot of misguided and even harmful love in the world. Even Paul felt the need to define love for the Corinthians. The problem lies in the fact that we are continually defining love in human terms—love with conditions, with strings attached. We say, "I love you because," "I'll love you if," or "I love you as long as . . ."

That kind of love will always bring heartache. The song is correct when it describes it as a "razor that leaves your soul to bleed." Bette Midler, however, has experienced a different kind of love. It is a miraculous love. She likens it to the miracle of a flower. A seed buried in dirt can be cold and frozen through the winter, yet it is still able to bloom in the spring. This kind of love can only come from God. We cannot earn such love, but can sow its seed. We must simply reach out and take it.

Follow It Up

"Evergreen," Barbra Streisand
"Home Inside of Me," Wes King

Russians

Sting (Sting)
The Dream of the Blue Turtle
A&M Records
1985—*Reached number 16*

Crank It Up

This song was written out of the Cold War fear that one day we would resort to a nuclear war. Even today, our global stupidity may still threaten our survival. Hopefully, before anyone pushes or activates any buttons we will look carefully at all our children's faces and see little difference in their smiles, whether they're from Maryland or Moscow.

Talk It Up

- Are you afraid of being in a war? Do you think you will see one soon? Why or why not?
- Why are our leaders so quick to resort to war as a solution? Is war ever necessary?
- What would you do if you thought our country was involved in an unjust war?
- Under what circumstances would you approve of your country using military power?
- Would you fight in a war if you were called by your country?

Look It Up

Psalm 68:30. Does this apply to modern nations? If so, how?

Ecclesiastes 3:8. Are you surprised to see this passage in the Bible? When would be the time for war? peace?

Luke 6:27–33. We know this verse applies to individuals; does it also apply to nations? What's the difference between what God commands for individuals and what he commands for nations?

Wrap It Up

Sting's song doesn't tackle the question of whether war is ever justified or whether individuals should serve their country by going to war. He does, however, challenge us to look carefully at the people we call our enemies. In doing so, he is echoing Jesus' words in Luke 6:27–33. If your enemy is an inanimate thing or an issue, it is easy to hate. When you hate, it is very easy to hurt or to engage in conflict. Sting urges us to look at our enemies as people who have the very same hopes, dreams, anxieties, and fears that we have, believing that so doing will help stop the conflicts.

Christ asks us to go even further. He asks us to love our enemies. To do that, we have no choice but to view them as people, which, of course, is what they are. They share the same Creator as us. When we fail to show them love, we fail to recognize God's image in them. Loving our enemies is the first step, and the biggest, toward peace and understanding.

Follow It Up

"War," Edwin Starr
"Eve of Destruction," Barry McGuire

 # Screen Door

● ● ● ● ● ● ● ● ● ● ●

Rich Mullins (Mullins)
Pictures in the Sky
Reunion
1987

Crank It Up

One of the major issues throughout the New Testament involves salvation . . . is it gained by faith or works? Or is it a blend of both? Can we enjoy our Lord without outward evidence of an inward commitment? Rich Mullins has some fun with these questions and throws in a catchy tune to boot.

Talk It Up

- Do you own anything that you rarely use? What?
- In what ways do you show your faith?
- Do you think some people pretend or play make-believe in showing their faith? If so, why?
- Do you ever put on a spiritual "show" for others?
- What actions should become natural outward signs of a deep commitment? Which are toughest for you?
- Where do you need to show your faith more? Around what people? How do you plan on doing this?

Look It Up

Ephesians 2:8–9. What does this passage say about works? Does it contradict what Rich Mullins says in his song? Why or why not?

James 2:14–26. What does this passage say about grace? Does it contradict what Ephesians 2:8–9 says? Why or why not? How can you reconcile these two passages?

Wrap It Up

Faith and works are key components of the Christian life. Trouble starts when people focus too strongly on one and exclude the other. It is easy to get caught up in works. We berate ourselves for not having daily devotions, for failing to memorize the Book of Micah, or for turning down the chance to build a church in the jungles of Africa.

On the other hand, a faulty understanding of grace can lead to spiritual laziness. We may discount the need for good works because we are saved by grace, not works. We think that good works may be important, but not vital.

What James—and Rich Mullins—are saying is that faith without works is not faith. True faith that comes from grace will produce works. It is the nature of that faith.

Are you trusting in Christ alone for your salvation (Eph. 2:8–9)? Examine your faith. Are you doing the works that should result from a saving faith (Eph. 2:10)? Examine your works.

Follow It Up

"What Have You Done for Me Lately?" Janet Jackson
"Sheep and Goats," Keith Green

 # Secret o' Life

• • • • • • • • • • • • •

James Taylor (Taylor)
JT
Columbia Records
1977

Crank It Up

"The secret of life," James Taylor sings, "is enjoying the passage of time." This simple little tune is unassuming enough. It does not delve into the meaning of life, explaining that even Einstein said "we could never understand it all." Since we can't understand it, Taylor reasons, "we might as well enjoy the ride."

Talk It Up

- How would you complete the phrase, "The secret of life is _____"? What do you think about the way James Taylor completes that phrase?
- If you could have any information about your future, what would you want to know?
- How would you change your life in the present?
- If you could relive any time in your past, what would you want to relive?
- How would it change your life in the present?

Look It Up

Matthew 6:25–34. What are things you worry about? Are you anxious about anything? How does God take care of you?

Philippians 4:4–9. What are ways you feel God's peace in your life? What specific things can you think about that fit verse 8?

Colossians 2:6–10. How can you let your roots grow deep in Christ? How might that affect what you think about the meaning of life?

Wrap It Up

In the three *Back to the Future* movies, Marty McFly (Michael J. Fox) frantically raced around the past and the future trying to protect his present. He was able to transform the past in order to improve the future. What a wonderful thing that would be. Few people would pass up the chance to change the past.

In another movie, *Peggy Sue Got Married,* Peggy Sue had that opportunity. By a quirk of fate, she was transported back to her high school days—with all the knowledge she had gained in the future. She was determined to use her knowledge to keep from making the same mistakes. To her dismay, however, she found herself making the mistakes all over again.

Of the two movies, *Peggy Sue Got Married* is probably more realistic, because the past is past. Even given the opportunity we probably couldn't change it. What we must do is come to terms with our past. Peggy Sue realized that being obsessed with her past would not change her future. She used her past to understand her present so she could enjoy life again.

God has given us a wonderful world to live in. Yet we hardly ever focus on the present. We spend our time agonizing over the past and planning our futures. We spend so much time in the past and future that we don't even realize what we are missing in the present.

When you gave God your life, you gave him your past, present, and future. Only he can give you a ride in the present that will surpass all your expectations. That is the secret of life.

Follow It Up

"Eagle Song," The Imperials
"More to This Life," Steven Curtis Chapman

Show Me the Way

Styx (DeYoung)
Edge of the Century
A&M Records
1990—*Reached number 3*

Crank It Up

For those familiar with old Styx songs, this tune places them in a new light. They are literally asking for guidance. In what many consider a blatantly Christian song, Styx is asking for someone to "wash my illusions away." Styx has voiced for many empty souls the desire to seek God and his abundant ways.

Talk It Up

- How did you become a Christian? Did someone explain the way to you? Were you comfortable with the answers they gave to your questions?
- Have you ever tried to "show the way" to someone else? How has your church and family background affected your feelings about witnessing?
- What would you say to someone who asked the questions Styx expresses in this song?
- Why do you think so many people are looking for answers? What have been some of the possible answers given to them by society?

Look It Up

John 3:1–22. How did Jesus "show the way" to Nicodemus? Would that explanation work today? Why or why not?

John 4:1–30. How did Jesus explain the way of salvation to the woman at the well? Why didn't he just explain it the way he did to Nicodemus?

Acts 8:26–39. How did Philip "show the way" to the Ethiopian? Were the Ethiopian's questions similar to the words of the Styx song? If so, how?

Acts 16:25–34. How did Paul and Silas "show the way" to the jailer? Could their approach ever work today? Why or why not?

Wrap It Up

It is not too often that someone sits down beside you and asks you to explain salvation. Yet here is a noted secular rock group doing that very thing.

God commanded us to grow spiritually so that we could go forth and be fishers of men. Far too often we expend our energies on growing instead of fishing. We need to spend more time bringing God's Word to the lost instead of hoarding it for ourselves.

To be a fisherman takes several elements. The first is presence. You can't catch a fish if you are not there to reel in the line. Isolated Christians worship, work, go to school, and play only with other Christians. It is rare that a complete stranger will be willing to sit and listen to you explain the gospel; people listen to those they respect and trust. Look at your life. Do you have contact with any non-Christians? Have you shared with them God's love? You need to put yourself out in the world to labor in the fields.

Second, you must earn respect and trust from those to whom you are witnessing. This means as you move out into the world, you must maintain your purity and holiness. Nothing turns people off faster than hypocrisy. People will only want what you have if they believe it is genuine.

Finally, you must know the way yourself. "Show Me the Way" is full of spiritual allusions and Christian jargon, yet the author still doesn't know the way. An astounding number of people know about God, Jesus, and the Bible. But they don't know the meaning of it all. Be sure you know the way. Study the Bible. Write out your testimony. Memorize key verses. It doesn't matter how you do it; what matters is *that* you do it. You must be ready. Make 1 Peter 3:15 your signature verse: "Always be ready to give a reason for the hope of glory within you."

Follow It Up

"Give Me Something to Believe In," Poison
"I Still Haven't Found What I'm Looking For," U2[*]

Shower the People

James Taylor (Taylor)
In the Pocket
Warner Bros. Records
1976—*Reached number 22*

Crank It Up

James Taylor takes the old theme of letting people know you care and gives it his own personal flair. In this song, one of his many popular tunes, Taylor reinforces the importance of not just loving people but letting them know how you feel. It's not enough to have good feelings; we must also act on them.

Talk It Up

- What are your favorite ways of showing people you love them? family? friends? teachers? Which of these get the best reactions?
- What are your favorite ways of being shown you are loved? Does it make a difference who it is? How does it make you feel?
- Do you ever find it difficult to "shower the people you love with love"?
- Are there any people you wish would show their affection more? In what ways? Who do you wish you could "shower" more often?
- How can you begin today to follow the advice of this song?

Look It Up

Romans 12:9–13. Do these verses relate to James Taylor's song? If so, how?

John 15:12–17. Does Jesus put any limits on our love? How do you think he would respond to this song?

Romans 6:23; Psalm 62:1–2. In what ways has God showered his affection on us? How can we follow his example?

Wrap It Up

James Taylor uses a powerful metaphor in this song. The idea of being showered with love would leave anyone breathless. When was the last time you felt totally and completely loved? When was the last time you showered someone with love?

Parents will often talk about that overwhelming feeling of love when they first hold their newborn child. Newlyweds bask in the warm glow of an emotion that has no equal. If love is such a powerful and desired emotion, one wonders why we find it so difficult to express.

One reason is that we've begun to take love for granted. We demand it. We feel it is owed us. Once we have it, we assume it is there permanently. We do not tend it. We don't realize how much we need it—until it is gone.

Another reason is that, slowly and subtly, our society has glorified self-sufficiency and self-reliance. People who are self-taught and self-made are held in high esteem, as if to say they are better because they didn't need other people. But even highly independent people need to be loved and encouraged. Our highest accolades should go to those people who know how to give and express love, not to those who seem to have no need of it.

Finally, we fail to shower people with love because we are afraid of rejection. In our minds, expressing love is not worth the risk of rejection. This is probably the most difficult fear to overcome. But Christ was continually rejected, and even denied by one of his closest friends—and he still showered people with love. He set the example and we are to follow it. As Christians, we need to shower people with God's unconditional love. It is that kind of a shower that will bring a lasting change.

Follow It Up

"Thank You for Being a Friend," Andrew Gold
"You've Got a Friend," James Taylor

 # Signs

• • • • • •

Five Man Electrical Band
Goodbyes and Butterflies
Lionel
1971—*Reached number 3*

Crank It Up

Sometimes we get tired of people telling us what to do. When signs tell us what to do, it infuriates us even more. This song talks about those signs we hate most—the ones that reveal our hypocrisy.

Talk It Up

- What issues are being covered with the signs in the song?
- What signs bother you the most? Why those?
- What signs (real or symbolic) are you putting up?
- What's the meaning of the song? Why does he write God a sign to tell him how he's doing?
- What sign would you like to write to God?

Look It Up

Matthew 7:1–2. In what ways do we judge others? How do you react when others judge you? Why do we tend to judge others more severely than we do ourselves?

Acts 10:34–35. Peter says "God does not show favoritism." What do you think he means?

1 Corinthians 10:12. What does this warning mean? How might it apply to our discussion?

Psalm 94:22. Why do you think the psalmist describes God as a refuge? How might that apply to our discussion?

Wrap It Up

Signs are everywhere. They tell us where to enter and to exit. They tell us who we should watch and what we should wear. They tell us what we can and can't do. As they multiply in number and in size, we tend to notice them less and less. There are some signs, however, that we never fail to notice.

We all have a number of signs, or labels, that we wear. Signs like "jock" or "student" describe our areas of interests. Other signs such as "quiet" or "outgoing" highlight our personality traits. Some signs, like "Christian" or "non-Christian," even describe our beliefs. There are two problems with such signs, however.

The first problem is that signs are one-dimensional; they describe us superficially. "Jock" is often accompanied by the word "dumb." "Quiet" often implies shy or backward. "Christian" sometimes suggests—to some people—straitlaced rule-makers with no sense of humor. Unfortunately, such judgments are almost always wrong.

The second problem occurs when we apply the signs to ourselves. We are often careless about the signs we choose, and even more careless about living up to them. It is our responsibility to represent ourselves honestly and consistently. When we call ourselves Christians, we take an awesome responsibility—of representing Christ to a fallen world. The more we do that, the more people will look for the Savior behind the signs.

Follow It Up

"Just the Way It Is," Bruce Hornsby and The Range[*]

# Snake in the Grass

Kim Hill (King)
Talk About Life
Reunion Records
1989

Crank It Up

Our deeds begin as seeds that, with proper mixtures of sun and rain, can mark our lives as significant. We are like farmers who plant seeds and wait for their full growth before harvest. This song from Kim Hill warns of those snakes that may come and take what was intended for good and turn it into something bad. We reap what we sow. As our seed matures, we are responsible to give it good growth cycles. Cutting back the weeds that strangle may be our best response, but beware of those snakes that come slithering low in the tall grass.

Talk It Up

- Are you afraid of snakes? Have you ever been bitten by one?
- Why does Kim Hill blame the snake for the evil the seed becomes?
- Why be afraid of the weeds? What kind of "weeds" do you have in your life?
- What kind of seed have you sown? Will you be satisfied with what you will reap?

Look It Up

Matthew 13. Study the four outcomes in the parable of the sower. Can you think of any modern parallels that fit the story? Do the same thing with the parable of the weeds in verse 24.

John 3:19–21. Why does evil hate light? What does the good deed doer have to fear? How do we keep our seed from being overtaken?

Wrap It Up

One of the goals of the appliance industry is to create products that require little or no maintenance. In our minds, time spent working on keeping something fit and running is time wasted. We even apply this maxim to our bodies. The market is saturated with exercise gadgets designed to produce fit bodies with a minimum of sweat and work.

There is great danger in this philosophy. It causes us to take things for granted. We begin to lose appreciation for the very things that serve to benefit us. We also begin to get lazy. When problems do arise, we are in a state of disbelief. We simply cannot understand how the problem could have happened. It is like a farmer walking through a field that he never mowed. As he strides along in the tall grass, he is bitten by a snake. He cannot figure out how he could have a snake in his field and how he could have been bitten.

Our spiritual lives are often like that field. If we do not tend them or take care to plant good seeds in them, they will become perfect hiding places for a snake. That snake is Satan. It is only by constant care and attention to our spiritual lives that we can be ready to face the snake. In *Walking on Water*, Madeleine L'Engle says we must pray even when it feels "dry as dust," for only by daily prayer can we be ready to pray when we really need God. Sometimes spiritual gardening does seem "dry as dust." Not every church service produces a spiritual high. Not every Sunday school class brings new and exciting insights. Not every quiet time leaves us feeling energized, poised for action. However, every church service, every Sunday school lesson, every quiet time does prepare you to meet the snake. When you tend your spiritual life with diligence, you will produce a rich harvest unharmed by the snake.

Follow It Up

"Dear John Letter to the Devil," Keith Green

 # So You Wanna Go Back to Egypt

• • • • • • • • • • • • • • • • • • •

Keith Green
Ministry Years 1980–1982, Vol. 2
Sparrow
1987

Crank It Up

Keith Green crafted this wonderful song about the Israelites' escape from Egypt. When the going got tough, they wanted to go back where it was safe and secure. With their constant whining, they provide a good example of what we look like when we fail to appreciate how well God has taken care of us.

Talk It Up

- What's the worst trip you've ever taken? What made it so bad?
- Are you a whiner? What makes you complain? In what ways are you like the Israelites? Are you better or worse than they?
- How has God taken care of you? Are you sometimes ungrateful? How do you show your appreciation to him?
- What things are you involved in now that you take for granted? Who do you need to thank for those activities?
- What do you need to do to ensure you're heading to Canaan and not Egypt?

Look It Up

Exodus 15:22–25; 16:2. Why did the children of Israel complain? What made them so blind to God's goodness? When do you complain? What makes you blind to God's goodness?

Matthew 20:20–28. What caused the disciples to whine? What was Jesus' response? How could they be "last"? How can you be "last" in today's world?

Wrap It Up

One of *Saturday Night Live's* most memorable skits depicted the "Whiners," a family that whined about everything in a high-pitched nasal voice that grated on the nerves. They whined if it was raining. They whined when the sun came out. They whined about the good and the bad. Adults across the country found it hilarious because, of course, they never sound like that. Or do they?

As much as we'd like to think otherwise, we haven't left behind the whines of our childhood. We're easily dissatisfied. Our patience is much too short. Pepsi's slogan expresses our childish self-centeredness: we "gotta have it," and we gotta have it right now! Two things happen when we buy into that philosophy.

First, we lose all the things we might have gained through patience. The Israelites were given a firsthand vision of the awesome power of the Lord as they were led out of Egypt. Daily, they got to see a tangible symbol of the Lord in the pillar of fire. Yet they would have thrown it all away to return to be slaves in Egypt.

Second, when we buy into the "gotta have it" mentality, we become willing to settle for second best as long as we can have it immediately. Our impatience results in lower standards. The Lord is capable of doing great things, things we never even thought of—if we wait on him.

So you wanna go back to Egypt? Think again. God's got better things in store for you.

Follow It Up

"I Am a Servant," Larry Norman*
"Almost Threw It All Away," Charlie Peacock

Started as a Whisper

Susan Ashton (Kirkpatrick and Simon)
Angels of Mercy
Sparrow Records
1992

Crank It Up

We live for information. Our appetite for knowledge has kept us moving forward in the pursuit of global excellence. Many of us have pushed the limits to know more, be more, experience more. From the Discovery Channel to the *National Enquirer,* we crave information and believe just about anything we hear. This song takes a look at what can happen when we believe what we hear about others. Gossiping can destroy people quicker than a bullet. Our tongues have damaged many a hurting person looking for respite and peace. What may start as a whisper ends up as a headline.

Talk It Up

- What have been some of the weirdest things you've heard lately as gossip?
- Do you know anyone whose life was destroyed by gossip? What were the repercussions?
- Have you ever "whispered" things that you wish you could take back? Were you able to fix the damage?
- Have people ever gossiped things about you that weren't true? How did it make you feel?
- How hard is it for you to keep quiet about things?
- What should we do when we can't control our tongue?

Look It Up

Matthew 12:36. What kinds of falsehood are we to stay away from?

Ephesians 4:29. What should your conversation accomplish?

Music Worth Talking About

Proverbs 18:8. What does this verse compare gossip to? Is it an accurate comparison? Why do we look for mean stories to pass along?

1 Timothy 4:7. Do you follow the command of this verse? How do you do it?

James 4:11. What does this verse say about a gossip?

Wrap It Up

Gossip is a vicious and deadly sin, yet it is everywhere. Friends, coworkers, and relatives engage in it without even thinking about it. Tabloid newspapers exist because of it. We have become so tolerant of it that we are immune to it. We often aren't even aware that we are gossiping.

One of the greatest dangers of gossip is that its damage cannot be undone. Whether the gossip is true or false, the hurtful words can never be erased. The hurt parties are never vindicated.

Another danger of gossip is that it engages us in a completely selfish act. We use the weaknesses or problems of others to try to feel good about ourselves. But God wants us to follow his example and share one another's burdens. He wants us to feel the pain of another. We can't do that if we are using their pain to feed our own fires of self-worth.

Finally, gossip prevents us from developing trusting relationships with other people. People who listen to our gossip understand that we could just as easily be talking about them. They cannot trust us.

Commit yourself this moment to stop speaking the words that hurt. Only speak what will be beneficial for others. If you have hurt someone, don't let the sun go down without making it right.

Follow It Up

"Harper Valley PTA," Bobbi Gentry
"Somebody Keeps Watching Me," Rockwell

 # Tears in Heaven

● ● ● ● ● ● ● ● ● ● ● ● ● ● ● ● ●

Eric Clapton (Clapton)
Rush
Reprise Records
1992—*Reached number 2*

Crank It Up

After his young son died in an accident, Eric Clapton went into a deep depression and questioned the meaning of life. But the memory of his son pulled him through. This song is about the young boy and what Clapton hopes will be a tearful reunion in heaven.

Talk It Up

- Who are you looking forward to seeing again in heaven? What will you talk about?
- Are there people you know that you are not sure you'll see in heaven? How does that make you feel?
- Are you assured that you will go to heaven when you die? If so, why? If not, how can you change that?

Look It Up

Matthew 5:3. What does it mean to be "poor in spirit"? Why do you think Jesus said the kingdom of heaven belongs to the poor in spirit?

Matthew 7:21. Who will go to heaven, according to this verse? What is the "will of the Father"?

1 Peter 1:3–4; Hebrews 10:34. What is reserved in heaven for us? What do you think that means?

Hebrews 12:23. Do you think God literally writes names down in a book? What does it mean to have your name written in heaven? Is your name written there? If so, how did it happen?

Wrap It Up

After two thousand years of research and speculation, scholars and theologians still find many aspects of Christianity a puzzle. While there is much we do understand, there seems to be even more that our human minds find difficult to grasp. We struggle with the idea of heaven and hell. We have endless questions. We want a heavenly travel brochure complete with pictures and testimonials.

While brochures might make us feel better, they couldn't do heaven justice. The wonders of heaven are beyond our human terms. We can only imagine the joy we will experience in heaven. It's the thought of that joy that gets us through the tough times.

Eric Clapton's four-year-old son fell to his death from an upper story window. Countless people throughout the centuries have experienced tragedies that have left them reeling from the pain. As the pain subsides, anger and questions arise. Often, the anger is directed at God.

When things are going well, we don't give God a thought. When tragedy strikes, we become angry at God for failing to intervene. But God, more than anyone else, cries with us in our pain. Yes, there are tears in heaven—tears of sadness as God weeps with us; but also tears of joy when we are reunited with loved ones and are restored to wholeness.

Follow It Up

"Thank You," Ray Boltz[*]

 # Thank You

• • • • • • • • • •

Ray Boltz (Boltz)
Thank You
Diadem
1988

Crank It Up

Ray Boltz sings this song about being a giver and not a taker—
a song about being involved, not detached; supportive, not
destructive; grateful, not unfeeling. We have no idea how many
people we touch by our lives. We need to see our interactions in
that respect—one smile, one word, or one gift may move another
soul heavenward.

Talk It Up

- How did you become a Christian? Did anyone influence that
  decision? Who? How?
- Who do you wish you could thank for their spiritual influence in your life? Who might want to thank you?
- What kinds of small things do you appreciate in others that
  usually go unnoticed?
- What do you do intentionally to let others know about your
  love for Jesus?
- What can you do this week to express gratitude to someone
  who has touched your life?

Look It Up

According to the following passages, when are we to give
thanks? What are some ways that we can give thanks to God?
What can we do to thank other people? Are they the same? Why
or why not?

Mark 8:6
Ephesians 5:20
2 Thessalonians 1:3

Philippians 4:6
1 Timothy 4:3
Psalm 95:2

Wrap It Up

If everyone in the world were to make a list of people who had touched his or her life, many people would be surprised at the names on the lists. We are often unaware of the impact we make on people. A simple smile or a small courtesy can change another person's day—and perhaps even his or her life. This song touches on two lessons.

The first is that Christians are to constantly touch the world around them. God's light needs to shine through our lives. Jesus tells us to be the salt of the earth and a light on a hill. We need to remember that as we go about our daily lives. We may never know the result of our good deeds, but God knows.

The second lesson is that we must learn to appreciate those who have had an impact on us. The Bible is full of admonitions to give thanks. We are told to "give thanks always," not only to God but to each other. We ought to thank the Sunday school teacher who took an interest in us, express our appreciation to the person whose witness led us to Christ, and show our gratitude to those who have given to us in big and small ways.

Follow It Up

"Testimony," Kim Hill
"Walk with the Wise," Steven Curtis Chapman
"Drowning Man," Charlie Peacock

 # They Killed Him

Bob Dylan (Kristofferson)
Knocked Out Loaded
Columbia Records
1986

Crank It Up

A quick look at our history tells us that many of our most beloved leaders had their lives ended in a brutal fashion. From Gandhi to John F. Kennedy, Robert Kennedy, Martin Luther King, and even Jesus, we seem to lose the instruments of hope and change when they are still young. This song echoes the shock, outrage, and disappointment we feel when someone we love is taken from us.

Talk It Up

- What great leader would you like to bring back from the dead to lead today? Why?
- Why are great leaders the targets of assassination? What purpose did their deaths serve?
- What can we do to prevent the loss of promising leaders? Will we ever be able to protect them?
- Why is Jesus' death not looked upon historically as a murder? What purpose did his death serve?

Look It Up

Matthew 15:19, 20. What other sins would you put in this list? Why do you think Jesus mentioned these specifically?

Acts 2:22–23. Did wicked men take Jesus' life or did he give it willingly? How was his death different from that of JFK or Martin Luther King?

1 Corinthians 15:1–8. How was Jesus' death part of God's plan for us?

John 10:10–11. What does Jesus want us to know about how he felt about dying?

Wrap It Up

"My God, they've killed him" is the chorus of this song. It conjures up all our anguish, disbelief, and outrage over each insane act. Why would anyone want to kill someone who is bringing about change for the better? This song wonderfully illustrates the senselessness of killing such people. Yet it also falls short. It relegates Jesus to the status of a great man who was assassinated.

Jesus' death was very different from the others. First, his life was totally blameless. Although the Kennedys, Martin Luther King, and Gandhi were great men, there were aspects to their lives that were less than respectable. Whispers of womanizing and adultery, self-preservation, and self-gratification swirled around these men. But Jesus was without blame.

Second, Christ's death had a purpose. The others' deaths were all senseless, leaving us wondering what might have been. Jesus' death was for the purpose of our salvation. He died so that we would have life and have it abundantly. It seems to be a harsh plan. How terrible and wonderful it was—terrible that God had to sacrifice his Son, but wonderful that he loved us enough to do it.

Follow It Up

"MLK," U2
"Abraham, Martin, and John," Dion

 # True Colors

Cyndi Lauper (Kelly and Steinberg)
True Colors
Portrait Records
1986—Reached number 1

Crank It Up

Sometimes we put ourselves into difficult spots when we hang around with hardened people. During these encounters we notice ourselves turning into people we don't want to become. Cyndi Lauper's uplifting song is about being ourselves, and the impact of having people around us who help us do just that. This song emphasizes the importance of genuineness and affirmation in a person's life. Using color to describe our personalities, Cyndi Lauper offers the challenge of letting your true colors shine through "like a rainbow."

Talk It Up

- What is your favorite color? Why? What is your least favorite color? Why?
- What does the phrase "true colors" represent in this song?
- What areas of your life right now accurately portray who you really are? What areas do not?
- What people give you freedom to be yourself? How do they do that?
- With what kinds of people do you enjoy hanging out? Why them? With whom do you wish you could spend more time? Why?

Look It Up

Psalm 139:1–24. In what ways does God know the true you? How do you benefit from this knowledge? Do you ever try to hide your true self from him? Does it work? Do you think he would love you more if he knew less about you?

185

Wrap It Up

Society places a high premium on the appearance of truth. It can make or break a politician. We want truth in advertising. Our justice system is based on discovering the truth. In fact, we demand truth in just about everything but ourselves.

Not only do we hide our true selves from others, but we often hide from ourselves. We bury our true colors so that no one can see what we're really like or what we really feel, until we're no longer sure ourselves of who we are.

But one person knows our real selves no matter what we try to do to hide. According to the psalmist, God is intimately acquainted with each of us. If God can know our true selves and still love us enough to send his Son to die for us, what have we to fear? Someone who is perfect loves us. It should not matter what someone who is imperfect thinks.

Once we experience God's love, we can begin to chip away at the shells we have placed around ourselves. Hiding our true selves will only distance us from the very love and acceptance we seek. As Cyndi Lauper says, "I see your true colors and that's why I love you."

Follow It Up

"Respect Yourself," Bruce Willis
"Chameleon Song," Lindy Hearn
"She Believes in Me," Kenny Rogers

 # Turning Thirty

• • • • • • • • • • • • •

Randy Stonehill (Stonehill)
Equator
Myrrh Records
1983

Crank It Up

As if reading from his personal journal, Randy Stonehill sings his feelings about being older. Rather than bemoan the effects of aging, he regards a new decade of life with a renewed sense of direction. Apparently happy with the person he's become, he promises to keep loving Jesus. This simple song gives insight into what really matters as we mature physically . . . family, friends, and faith.

Talk It Up

- Name your favorite birthday so far. Why was it so special?
- How do you feel about getting older? Are you happy to be your age or are you impatient to be older? Why?
- How have you changed in the past five years? What new insights have you gained?
- What kinds of things are you looking forward to when you are in your thirties? forties? fifties?
- How would you grade yourself with how you've done so far in life? How do you think God would grade you?

Look It Up

Titus 2:2, 6. What qualities should Christian men possess?
Titus 2:3–5. What qualities should Christian women possess?
Proverbs 3:4–6. What should we be doing with our lives no matter what age we are? Is that hard now? Will it get easier as you get older?

Proverbs 22:6. What patterns have been set in your life that keep you in the grace of God? What patterns need to be acquired? Will you be ready for the final hour?

Wrap It Up

Everyone's life is full of milestones. There are physical milestones, such as learning to walk, starting school, and graduation. There are personal milestones, such as our first love and our first job. There are legal milestones as well. When you are sixteen, you can drive. When you are eighteen, you can vote. There is one set of milestones, however, that we give little attention—our spiritual milestones.

Most Christians can recall at least one spiritual milestone— when they became a Christian. Other than that, they don't keep track of important events in their spiritual lives. They assume that once they believe the process is finished. But Christianity is not a one-event journey. It is full of milestones just as any other developmental process. Think about your spiritual milestones. What events have moved you along? Who has influenced you? What books have encouraged your growth? What spiritual abilities have you developed?

Next, dream about directions you want to go. What spiritual gifts do you desire? What new abilities do you want to develop? The exciting thing about Christianity is that the growth process is never finished. God can take you places you never dreamed. You just have to keep moving, year after year.

Follow It Up

"Like a Rock," Bob Seger
"The Great Adventure," Steven Curtis Chapman[*]

Twenty Years Ago

Kenny Rogers (Rogers)
They Don't Make 'Em Like They Used To
RCA Records
1986

Crank It Up

Kenny Rogers sings about life twenty years ago and wonders whether it was easier then than now. We've gone from small ice cream shops on two-lane main streets to huge malls off the interstate; we now have the benefits (and the dangers) of global access and computer age communications. This song suggests that we've let progress invade our living arrangements to the point where it now controls us, rather than us controlling it. Kenny also feels the personal pain of lost friendships and lost traditions. He knows that his once simple outlook on life has gotten more complicated. We feel the weight of a man recognizing how he has changed over the years, maybe not for the better.

Talk It Up

- What age in your life would you like to go back and revisit? Why?
- What kinds of stories do your parents tell you about life when they were children?
- Do you think society is better off now than twenty years ago? Why or why not?
- Are you a better person now than you were five years ago? one year ago? What do you think you'll be like five years from now?

Look It Up

Psalm 139:1–24. In what ways does God know us?
Ecclesiastes 3:15. How does God view our past?

189

Wrap It Up

Kenny Rogers' song is nostalgic. We all tend to look at the past through rose-colored glasses. The past was simpler, slower, better. Yet the past also had its share of tragedies, including two world wars and the Korean and Vietnam wars. Twenty years ago was a time of economic downturns and energy crises. Families were in trouble as far back as the turn of the century. So why, then, do we idealize the past? Perhaps it is because we are afraid of the future. People who live without hope for the future have to have something to believe in. They tend to turn to something comfortable and familiar, such as the past. Yet, it is a past remembered without the bad parts.

Wishing to be back in the past will not help in the future. As it says in Ecclesiastes 3:15, "Whatever is has already been, and what will be has been before." There is nothing wrong with examining the past. It is a part of who we are. However, only as we take that understanding of ourselves and rise up to meet God's future are we truly living today.

Follow It Up

"Memories," Barbra Streisand
"Paper in Fire," John Cougar Mellencamp*
"Boy in the Bubble," Paul Simon
"Old Man," Neil Young

Two out of Three Ain't Bad

Meatloaf (Steinman)
Bat out of Hell
Epic Records
1977—*Reached number 11*

Crank It Up

This '70s tune was pegged as a love story. Its soothing melody and sensitive tune have all the trappings of a romantic ballad until you listen to the words. "I want you. I need you. But there ain't no way I'm ever going to love you. Don't be sad, because two out of three ain't bad." In the verses, Meatloaf sings of an earlier love to whom his heart was given. He was asked by this love to accept "two out of three," and now, in turn, he is asking someone else to accept his less-than-perfect offer. Having felt the pain of not getting everything he wants in a relationship, Meatloaf expresses willingness to inflict similar pain on someone else.

Talk It Up

- When did you fall in love for the first time?
- What qualities does true love have?
- Have you ever been in Meatloaf's position (of accepting less than the best in a relationship)?
- What do you think people want out of relationships? Are they usually willing to put the same into them? Why or why not?
- Why do relationships end?

Look It Up

1 Corinthians 13:4–8. For each of the characteristics of love listed in this passage, identify an action that would show that characteristic. Try to rank the characteristics from most important to least. Which, if any, of the characteristics, could you do without? Which of the characteristics does the world most often overlook?

Wrap It Up

If they ever did a research study on song topics, love would certainly be the number one topic. Another study might look at the evolution of love songs over the years. Such a study would undoubtedly show that love songs have changed from tender declarations and pledges of commitment to songs centered on the physical aspects of love.

With one out of every three marriages ending in divorce, and the entertainment industry portraying shallow, temporary relationships, we are no longer able to give anyone a true picture of love. People have confused love with security. The need for commitment is completely ignored. The failure of love to meet one's expectations is grounds for termination. The focus of love has shifted from the other person to the self.

First Corinthians 13 portrays love as completely unselfish. It is love that seeks to uplift and protect the other person. None of the verses talk of what the bestower of that love expects. This is the true love that everyone is seeking. It is a gift from God. Only when we accept the Creator of this love can we turn around and give it to someone else. In short, two out of three *is* bad. It is not enough to want someone, nor even to need someone; we will only know fulfillment when we learn to truly love another.

Follow It Up

"I Honestly Love You," Olivia Newton John
"What's Forever For?" Michael Murphey*

 # UFO

• • • • •

Larry Norman (Norman)
In Another Land
Word
1976

Crank It Up

Larry Norman sings about Jesus coming back to earth like a UFO, unidentified to those who don't know him. Upon his return, he will take his followers away and leave behind those who denied his existence. This classic Norman tune is a favorite of the many who enjoy thinking of the day of Jesus' return.

Talk It Up

- Have you ever seen a UFO?
- Do you think there is life on other planets? Why or why not? What could be the explanation for UFOs?
- What do you think about Norman's statement, "If there is life on other planets, he's been there once already and has died to save their souls"?
- When do you think Jesus is coming back? Are you ready?
- What do you think it will be like? What will earth be like an hour after he leaves?
- Does the prospect of his return scare you? Why or why not?

Look It Up

Matthew 25:1–13. What is the meaning of this parable? What does the oil represent? What does the banquet stand for? When will the hour of his return be?

Matthew 25:31–46. What is the meaning of this parable? What things should we be doing to get ready for his return? What is the difference between sheep and goats? How should we prepare for his return?

Wrap It Up

One aspect of Christianity that many people struggle with is the concept of the unsaved not going to heaven. Our view of a loving God is in conflict with the idea of a judging God. People say, "He led a good life. He was a good man. Surely he will go to heaven." Paul made it very clear that we are saved by grace, not works (see Eph. 2:8–9). It is our belief and commitment that determines our entrance into glory. The idea of God sending someone to hell seems harsh, but it is biblical. In Matthew 10:32–34, Jesus talks of the consequences of our disowning God. He describes himself as bringing a sword. There is another image of the Lord besides a benevolent Creator. It is one of a righteous Judge.

The picture is not meant to scare us into accepting God's grace. It is simply a statement of the facts. If we accept God's grace by believing in him and committing ourselves to his Son, we are assured of glory when his kingdom comes. If we choose not to accept his grace, the consequences are clear.

For the sheep, of course, it is not enough to be ready ourselves; we must help others get ready. How terrible it will be if on judgment day one of our friends turns to us and asks, "Why didn't you tell me? How could you not tell me?" Indeed, how can we not tell them? If the idea of others being condemned to hell bothers us so much, we should do something about it. It is our task to tell the world the Good News. When Christ returns, everyone should know exactly who he is.

Follow It Up

"The Sheep and the Goats," Keith Green
"I Wish We'd All Been Ready," Larry Norman
"People Get Ready," Rod Stewart*

 # Up on the Roof

● ● ● ● ● ● ● ● ● ● ● ● ● ●

James Taylor (Goffin and King)
Flag
Columbia Records
1979—*Reached number 28*

Crank It Up

This song is about getting away from the pressures of this world. With our travel to the roof, we are able to put things into proper perspective. When we look at things in a more peaceful setting, we realize they are not worth worrying about. The roof shouldn't be a permanent resting place, but with occasional visits, the roof can be a great place to refocus and recharge our batteries.

Talk It Up

- Where is your favorite vacation spot? Why? Where would you like to go? Why?
- How do you manage to get away from your worries? Where is your "roof"?
- What kinds of worries do you have?
- What worries have you had in the past? Did the thing(s) you worried about come to pass?
- Is it better to escape your worries or confront them?

Look It Up

Matthew 14:13. Why was it important for Jesus to be alone sometimes?

Matthew 14:23, 24. What did Jesus do when he was alone? What other things might he have done alone?

John 11:54. Why did Jesus take the disciples with him in this instance?

Psalm 121. How does this psalm apply to you and your worries?

195

Wrap It Up

During the '70s, a national hotel chain marketed a weekend package that included a two-night stay and discounts on meals. It was aimed at local residents, not travelers. The chain called it an "Escape Weekend." The goal was for local couples to escape from the pressures of daily living in the luxury of a hotel.

We all need to escape at times. Sometimes it is needed for purely physical reasons. The day-to-day aspects of living may cause actual physical fatigue; the escape is needed to rejuvenate the body. When the escape is over, the body is energized and ready to go.

Another reason to escape is to overcome mental fatigue. Sometimes our thoughts become jumbled and our minds burdened. During the escape, our burdens are cast aside and we focus on the pleasures of life. As our spirits lighten, we feel better prepared mentally to pick up the burdens once again.

Sometimes people escape simply to gain a new perspective. When you are in the midst of a situation, it is often difficult to see the whole picture. You get bogged down by details. You need to get away from the situation and view it from afar. That way, you can see what is important and what is trivial. You can refocus and renew your purpose based on the new perspective. Up on the roof you can see how the tree fits in the whole park. Even Jesus needed to go "up on the roof" from time to time.

Follow It Up

"Cool Change," Little River Band*
"Sailing," Christopher Cross

 # Used to Be

• • • • • • • • • • •

Stevie Wonder (Wonder and Charlene)
Used to Be
Motown Record Co.
1982—Reached number 46

Crank It Up

This song was on the pop charts in the early '80s. It refers to several events of that time. The phrase, "Superman was killed in Dallas" refers to the assassination of President Kennedy. Later in the song, "There's no love left in the palace," refers to an incident at Buckingham Palace, in which a man sneaked past the guards and wandered into Queen Elizabeth's bedroom. The man later revealed to the tabloids that the Queen and her husband, Prince Philip, slept in separate bedrooms.

After allusions to other such events, the song talks about the importance of love in the world. "Someone tried to say it once and they nailed him to a tree," the lyrics say, ending with, "I guess it's still the way it used to be."

Talk It Up

- If this song were written today, what current events do you think would be included?
- Do you think the song ends on a hopeful note? Why or why not?
- Do you think it is "still the way it used to be"? Why or why not?
- Is it useless to try to spread love in today's world? Why or why not?

Look It Up

1 Thessalonians 5:1–10. What does this passage mean by talking about being people of the light and people of the day? Does this passage relate to the song? If so, how?

197

John 15:9–17. Why did Jesus command us to love each other?
How do we "remain" in God's love?

John 16:33. What gives us hope to deal with the troubles in the
world? What does Jesus mean when he says he has overcome the world?

Wrap It Up

When we look around us at all of the problems in the world,
it's easy to think there is nothing we can do to really have an
impact or make a difference. When famines and disasters strike,
or wars break out, we feel small in comparison and incapable of
doing anything to help. If all we do is look at the scope of the
problems, then the song is correct. Things are still the way they
used to be.

But because Jesus came into the world, things are not the way
they used to be. There are people out there spreading God's love.
Their actions may be small and not easily noticed, or not considered newsworthy by the media. But they are nonetheless making an impact on people's lives. All of us need to take part in
spreading God's love throughout our world. We need to live and
share God's love in our daily lives as Christ showed us. Only then
will our world be changed.

Follow It Up

"American Pie," Don McLean
"Sign o' the Times," Prince

 # Vincent

● ● ● ● ● ● ● ●

Don McLean (McLean)
American Pie
EMI Records Group North America
1971—*Reached number 12*

Crank It Up

This song explores the reasons why Vincent Van Gogh committed suicide. We are shocked that anyone could be so desperate to consider suicide, but when it's someone famous, we find it even harder to believe. Don McLean's lyrics explore the intimate pain that Van Gogh must have felt.

Talk It Up

- Do you know anyone personally who has committed suicide? How did you react to their death?
- Do you know of any famous people who have committed suicide?
- Have you ever thought about ending your life? What brought you to that point? What keeps you from doing it?
- Does suicide affect only the individual? How does it affect others?

Look It Up

1 Corinthians 3:16, 17. Do these verses relate to suicide? If so, how?
1 Corinthians 6:19. What does this say about how we should treat our bodies?
2 Corinthians 6:16. Does suicide solve any problems? What does this passage say about God and his ability to help us in (and through) our problems?

Wrap It Up

Everyone goes through struggles. We all face tough times when self doubt, depression, and fear rule our lives. We all feel desperate at times. But it is difficult for most of us to imagine a pain so deep that death becomes an option. Yet there are people out there contemplating that option every day.

After a person has succeeded in ending his life, his friends and family spend hours berating themselves for failing to help him. They wonder if they could have prevented the tragedy. The truth of the matter is that we cannot heal a pain that deep. Only God is capable of healing such a wound. We need to be the instrument through which God can display his peace. We need to direct the hurting person to God in order to relieve the pain.

If you know someone contemplating suicide, let someone know—a minister, teacher, parent, or friend. If you are contemplating suicide, please do two things—*talk* to someone and *turn* to God. Accept help from someone else; accept healing from God himself.

Follow It Up

"Annie," Petra
"You're Only Human (Second Wind)," Billy Joel*

What's Forever For

• • • • • • • • • • • • • • • • • •

Michael Martin Murphey (Van Hoy)
The Best of Michael Martin Murphey
EMI Records Group North America
1982—*Reached number 19*

Crank It Up

The divorce rate continues to climb and its not unusual to hear of even well-respected couples having difficulty working things out together. Our families are being crippled from the destruction that divorce brings. We have begun to question the purpose of marriage. More and more people are simply living together to distance themselves from any pain that might come their way because of a marriage license. It's no surprise that this song asks the question, If marriages and love aren't forever, then what's forever for?

Talk It Up

- Are you or any of your friends from split homes? How has divorce affected you (them)?
- Why are so many families breaking up? What keeps families together?
- What will you do to ensure that your marriage will be a life-long commitment?
- How will your faith in God help you keep your commitment?

Look It Up

Genesis 2:18 and *Matthew 5:32*. Why do people get married?
Matthew 19:4–12. Under what circumstances is divorce permitted by Jesus? Does that make it easier for the people involved? Why or why not?

Romans 7:2–4. What does this passage teach about divorce? What would Paul say about today's standards? Does this also fit the spirit of Jesus' words on forgiveness? If so, how?

Wrap It Up

One of the saddest aspects of today's culture is the casual tolerance of divorce. It has become an acceptable option in the presence of strife and trouble. Although most couples don't think of divorce as an option when they get married, one wonders whether they marry seriously thinking about commitment in all circumstances. In her book *Walking on Water,* Madeleine L'Engle said that in her marriage there were times when she did not love her husband (actor Hugh Franklin), but she was always committed to him.

One of the most precious gifts God gives us is marriage. He gives us the chance to spend a lifetime with another soul, bonded in love and companionship. Who would turn down such a gift? Not many. But are you willing to work for it? God never promised that our love in marriage would remain constant forever. It ebbs and flows with life's twists and turns. Only love based on commitment can ride out the storm.

This type of love in marriage parallels our relationship with God. We don't simply say "I love you, God" and stop there. We commit ourselves to him. This act of commitment binds us to God forever. So, too, in marriage it is the act of commitment that binds us together and keeps us moving. Committing ourselves to a lasting love that is God-given—that's what forever is for.

Follow It Up

"Love and Marriage," Frank Sinatra
"You Don't Bring Me Flowers," Neil Diamond/Barbra Streisand

Where Do the Children Play?

Cat Stevens (Stevens)
Tea for the Tillerman
A&M Records
1970

Crank It Up

This song is about what happens when we put all our effort into progress and forget that we also need places for children to play. How many parks have been covered up for apartment complexes? Will we eventually lose our natural resources and game preserves to parking lots and shopping centers? Stevens wrote this song about ecology and the environment before these issues became politically correct.

Talk It Up

- Where is your favorite park? What kinds of play equipment does it have? What's your favorite part of the park?
- How do you feel about recycling? Do you separate your trash? Why or why not?
- Do you think we've become too fixated on progress? Should we be more concerned about ecology?
- Are you for preserving city parks? Would you like to have more neighborhood parks? Would you be willing to pay extra for that privilege for children?

Look It Up

Genesis 1. What responsibilities were given to us concerning this earth? Do you think God still thinks his earth is good?
Luke 16:1–12. Jesus spoke this parable about men who had been given responsibility. How did they respond? How are you responding to your charge to "fill the earth and subdue it" (Gen. 1:28)? How can you do better?

203

Wrap It Up

A series of futuristic movies were made in Australia in the '80s featuring a character named Mad Max. Mad Max was continually fighting the evil villains who ran rampant in a desecrated world. The landscape was barren because of a destroyed ozone layer. Great trash heaps dotted the countryside. Few people had cars or heat due to the depletion of natural fuels. Life was a constant struggle for survival because of humanity's total destruction of the world's resources. That barren world was just one filmmaker's vision of the future, but many people fear that it may not be too far off the mark.

The '90s have become the decade of the environment. Organizations encourage recycling. Scientists work to find alternatives to natural resources. Activists fight to save animals and nature. Our government has begun to impose stricter environmental regulation. Is it enough to stop the destruction?

We seem to be a people given to misuse of God's creation. In the '70s, during the energy crisis, President Carter urged Americans to conserve. We did well for a while. Most cars seen on the road were economy cars. People carpooled to work. Lights were turned off. Few people decorated with outside lights at Christmas. As a nation, we pulled together in a crisis. Unfortunately, the crisis point passed and we eased up on our sacrifices. Even though scientists are alarmed at the rate fuel is being consumed, we are back to driving big cars and vans. Elaborate light displays are common at Christmas. Thoughts of conservation have gone out the window.

As Christians, we need to make drastic changes in our attitudes and not wait for another crisis point. From the moment of creation, God placed us in charge of the plants and animals. He assured us that he would take care of us, but commanded us to be caretakers of the earth. Without our homes, we would become nomads. But without the earth, we become extinct. Preserve your corner for you and those who follow.

Follow It Up

"Teach Your Children Well," Crosby, Stills, and Nash
"Who'll Stop the Rain?" Creedence Clearwater Revival

Why Should the Devil Have All the Good Music?

●●●●●●●●●●●●●●●●●●●●●●●●●●

Larry Norman (Norman)
Only Visiting This Planet
Phydeaux Records
1972

Crank It Up

In this classic, Larry Norman sings about his disdain for the box people put him and his music in. He sings loud and clear that Christian music doesn't have to be second-rate and all of it doesn't have to be slow and melodically soothing. With his amps turned on full blast, he cranks out his answer to the question, What kind of music would Jesus play if he were a master musician today? If it weren't for Larry and his contemporaries, we still might be listening to only organs and harps as we sit in the pews on any given Sunday. Being a Christian and a musician should blend easily, and the musical styles should be as varied as the people who listen to the music.

Talk It Up

- What kind of music do you enjoy listening to before school? after dinner? before games? during parties? at church?
- What musicians would you most want to see perform in concert?
- What songs would your church have problems using in a Sunday worship service that you would want to hear? Why would there be a problem?
- What makes a song a Christian song? A non-Christian song? Do we need the labels "Christian" and "non-Christian"? Why or why not?
- How would you feel about Metallica singing a Sandi Patti song or Michael W. Smith singing a Van Halen tune?

- Do you think God is ever offended by our musical choices? Why or why not?
- How do you discern "good" songs from "bad" ones?

Look It Up

> *2 Samuel 6:5; 1 Chronicles 15:28; Psalm 33:1–3.* What words in these verses give you the idea that the music was not peaceful and soothing? In these verses, how is music used (what's the purpose)?

Wrap It Up

This song addresses the age-old question, What is holy? The Bible is filled with exhortations to be holy and examples of holy living. Because the Bible is timeless, it does not address specific issues unique to today. Many Christians want everything to be black and white, right or wrong, with no gray areas. It is difficult, if not impossible, to do this. The issues must be studied through the Word and prayer so that God can give you the wisdom to make the right choices.

With regard to music, the issue is not easy. Music itself is not sinful although the lyrics may be sinful. The ability to make music is a gift from God. Not all who possess the gift choose to glorify God with it. Even those who claim to glorify God with their music sometimes misuse the gift for self-glorification. God can be glorified in music even though the musician did not intend it to be so.

The question is, How do you determine which is which? In Romans 14:22, Paul tells us that such matters are "between you and God." The danger is that most of the music we hear we don't really listen to. Radios are on, songs rise to the top of the charts, and the world sings the chorus in the shower without ever understanding what the song is really saying. People need to listen to the words and understand the message before determining the holiness of the music.

Follow It Up

"God Gave Rock and Roll to You," Petra

Wind Beneath My Wings

Bette Midler (Henley and Silbar)
Beaches
Atlantic Records
1989—*Reached number 1*

Crank It Up

There are people in our lives who make living so much easier. They help us to be more than we could otherwise be. They ask nothing in return. They only want to see us fly. The beauty of Bette Midler's voice turns this song into a gift for our personal heroes.

Talk It Up

- If you could be anybody in the world for one day, who would it be? Why that person? Who would you pick if you could be somebody in your family for a day? in your school?
- Who's the one person you most enjoy talking to? Why that person? How do they inspire you?
- What's the best thing anyone has ever done for you? In what ways have others made your life better? What sacrifices did they make? Have you thanked them? How?
- What people do you give encouragement to? Why those people? How do you inspire them? How do they thank you?

Look It Up

Philippians 2:1–11. What kinds of things are we to do for each other? How much of this goes on in your life now? When have you had someone else encourage you this way?

Ephesians 4:1–3. Can you think of anyone who exhibits these characteristics? Describe that person. Does he or she inspire others? In what ways?

Ephesians 4:29–32. How often do you act this way? What holds you back from doing it more?

Acts 4:36. Barnabas was such a great friend to others that he was known by a nickname that meant "son of encouragement." What nickname would others give to you to express your best quality? What names might you give to some of your friends to highlight their positive traits?

Wrap It Up

If you ever have arrived at a concert early, you may have been surprised at the number of people bustling around getting things ready. Stage hands set up microphones. Musicians tune instruments. An electrician works the lights. Another person tests the sound-board. All of this is done so that one performer (or a group) can come out and shine. At the end of the concert thousands of people will applaud for the performer. Comments regarding his talent or her skill will fly back and forth. Rarely will someone comment on how nice the lighting was. All the people who worked behind the scenes are simply overlooked. They are like shadow people.

Shadow people are those people who stay in the background working to provide support and encouragement so that someone else may shine. These people are seldom recognized, publicly or privately. Yet there are more shadow people in the world than spotlight people, and they are absolutely vital to other people's success.

We give favor to certain gifts such as singing, acting, preaching, or speaking, and overlook other gifts, such as organizing, editing, and even encouraging. We need to acknowledge that all gifts are valuable. The spotlight needs to focus on the sound man from time to time. We need to acknowledge and thank those in our background whose gifts support us.

We also need to accept that we might be shadow people. We need to examine and develop our gifts and use them fully. Our place in the lives of others is extremely important. We free people from restraints that may hold them back. We voice encouragement when others need to hear it. We are valuable to their development as people. There is no purpose in the world greater than loving others. When we lift someone else to new heights, we become the wind beneath their wings.

Follow It Up

"Thank You for Being a Friend," Andrew Gold
"Thank You," Ray Boltz*

 # You're Only Human (Second Wind)

Billy Joel (Joel)
Greatest Hits, Vols. I and II (1973–1985)
Columbia Records
1985—Reached number 9

Crank It Up

This is Billy Joel's answer to the thousands who feel like their lives have not amounted to much and want to commit suicide. During these times of despair his suggestion is to wait for that second wind . . . after all, you're only human. Problems happen to even the best of us; that's no reason to end your life.

Talk It Up

- What kind of funeral would you want?
- Have you ever contemplated suicide? Why?
- What does it mean to "get your second wind"?
- What parts of your life are too valuable to end?
- What parts of yourself would you like to change?

Look It Up

The following passages deal with heroic Bible characters doing some surprising, imperfect things. For each passage, discuss what made the character righteous and heroic. Then discuss what happened in the passage. Finally, discuss what the character was feeling as he let God down.

2 Samuel 11 and *12:1–13* (David and Bathsheba)
Judges 16 (Samson and Delilah)
John 18:15–27 (Peter)

Wrap It Up

The video for "You're Only Human" has Billy Joel portraying an angel speaking to a young man about to commit suicide. His words seem simple: "You're only human." In other words, you will make mistakes. Things won't go perfectly. He goes on to suggest that things will get better. You will get a "second wind."

How true this is. Look at the Bible characters listed above. All three were very respected and righteous men. All three sunk about as low as man could go. When they came to their senses, they must have felt unbearable pain, the kind of pain that makes you want to give up. Not one of the three did give up. All of them worked through their pain and gained a second wind. David continued to expand and strengthen his godly kingdom. Jesus was descended from David's line. Samson redeemed himself by bringing down the temple on the heads of the Philistines. Peter went on to start the Christian church. How different history would be if they chose to end their lives to ease their pain.

In our own lives there will be pain also. At times it may be so great that we may want to put an end to it. However, we are no different from David, Samson, and Peter. We are human. We will make mistakes. Our expectations need to be realistic if we are to end the pain. Billy Joel is right; things will get better. In the meantime, we need to find more positive ways to deal with our pain. David and Samson spent a lot of time in prayer. Peter jumped into action. He continued to do the work Jesus had started.

The bottom line is that we are human. We are created by God. That in and of itself is worth living for. God deeply cares for his creation. He is with us through all our pain. Without him, there is no reason for living. With him, there is every reason to wait for that second wind.

Follow It Up

"Vincent," Don McLean*
"Almost Threw it All Away," Charlie Peacock

Index of Topics

(songs are arranged alphabetically in book)

211

Index of Artists

● ● ● ● ● ● ● ● ● ● ● ● ● ● ●

Index of Scripture

● ● ● ● ● ● ● ● ● ● ● ● ● ● ● ● ● ●